5 Minutes with Jesus

Quiet Time for Your Soul

Sheila Walsh

with Sherri Gragg

THOMAS NELSON
Since 1798

5 Minutes with Jesus: Quiet Time for Your Soul

Published in Nashville, Tennessee, by Thomas Nelson. Thomas Nelson is a registered trademark of HarperCollins Christian Publishing, Inc.

Cover design by Katie Jennings Design

Thomas Nelson titles may be purchased in bulk for educational, business, fund-raising, or sales promotional use. For information, please e-mail SpecialMarkets@ ThomasNelson.com.

ISBN-13: 978-0-7180-3259-3
ISBN-13: 978-1-4041-0753-3 (custom)

Printed in China
18 19 20 21 22 DSC 6 5 4 3 2 1

Introduction

Each year in amusement parks all over the world, thousands of us line up to ride the most gravity-defying, adrenaline-inducing thrill rides we can find. Giddily, we wait in line for our turn and then, at last, buckle up for the ride. Few of us pay attention to the bored sixteen-year-old at the control panel—even though he's the one with access to the large red emergency stop button, the last safeguard in the rare event that the ride goes too fast, spins a little too wildly, and hurtles out of control.

Have you ever wished you had a stop button for your life?

I sure have. Some days my life feels like a thrill ride that has slipped past fun and into the realm of chaos. It's an easy place to be in our modern world. Gone are simpler, quieter days when evenings were spent visiting with neighbors on the front porch or with family around the dinner table. Now blinking screens and beeping notifications have been added to the menu of never-ending entertainment options able to fill every waking moment of the daylight hours and even jar us from our sleep at night.

As if that were not all exhausting enough, if you're like me, you sometimes feel as if you never, ever stop running from one activity to another.

Is it any wonder we are anxious and deeply weary? We simply were not made to live like this—running full-tilt, dashing through one adrenaline-fueled day to another against a soundtrack created by phone calls, e-mails, texts, computers, TV, radio, and even on occasion, in-person human voices.

Isn't it time we hit the emergency stop button even for just a few minutes?

Well, friend, this is the invitation I am offering you today: the chance to step off the thrill ride of life and into the arms of your loving Savior. He waits to lead you beside still waters that will refresh your soul and to green pastures where you will find rest (Psalm 23).

God loves you. He never intended for you to live a frenzied, exhausting life. Listen to the words of Psalm 127:2: "It's useless to rise early and go to bed late, and work your worried fingers to the bone. Don't you know he enjoys giving rest to those he loves?" (THE MESSAGE).

Jesus longs to give you the gift of rest, and it can begin with five minutes a day . . .

Five minutes to shut out the noise . . .

Five minutes to find peace in the midst of a troubled world . . .

Five minutes to step out of the crosshairs of a culture that constantly demands more, more, and more . . .

Five minutes to receive God's sweet rest for your soul.

What do you say?

If you could use a little support along the way, come join the community we've been building at 5MinuteswithJesus.com, where you can find encouraging videos, images to share, and other reminders that just five minutes a day can transform our lives. We'd love to have you join us as we help each other keep turning to Jesus every day.

Are you ready to hit that stop button?

As a Mother
Comforts Her Child

It seemed to sneak up on me overnight. One moment Christian was a little boy who needed his mom for so much, and the next he was off to college—independent, confident, and strong.

One morning I sat in my favorite chair with a cup of tea, looking through old family photo albums and remembering some of my favorite moments from his childhood. There was the Alaska trip when Christian was nine years old. Part of our trip package included dogsledding. The chief "musher" asked Christian if he would like to direct the sled. When Christian looked at me, I said, "Go for it! You can do it. If you fall, I'll be right there."

I must have said that a hundred times as he was growing up: "If you fall, I'll be right there!" Now I say a variation of it in my prayers for him, thanking God that if Christian falls, his heavenly Father will be right there.

We can find great comfort in thinking of God as our Father. But did you know that when God wanted to describe how He comforts His children, God compared Himself to a mother?

In the book of Isaiah, God had some difficult things to say to His children, the Israelites. Despite His loving care of them, they had stubbornly rejected Him over and over again. He had sent His messengers, the prophets, to call His children back to Him, but they didn't listen. Finally, the time came when the Lord decided to let His children have their own way.

But the Israelites had forgotten something important: the same God they were rejecting was the One protecting them. He warned the Israelites that when He removed His protection, their enemies would sweep in and take them into captivity. It was terrifying, heartbreaking news—and God knew it. He couldn't bear to deliver it without comforting His children, and when He did, He used this imagery: "As a mother comforts her child, so will I comfort you" (Isaiah 66:13).

One of the most precious blessings of taking time to replenish our souls in God's presence is the tender comfort He offers us when we are hurting. It is so easy to run to a thousand other places when our hearts are wounded, but our compassionate God wants us to come to Him. He wants us to trust Him with our wounded hearts.

Will you allow Him to comfort you today?

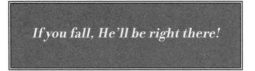

If you fall, He'll be right there!

∼⦿ Five Minutes in the Word ⦿∼

Comfort, comfort my people, says your God.

Isaiah 40:1

*You who bring good news to Jerusalem, lift up your voice with a shout,
lift it up, do not be afraid; say to the towns of Judah, "Here is your God!"*

Isaiah 40:9

*He tends his flock like a shepherd: He gathers the lambs in his arms and
carries them close to his heart; he gently leads those that have young.*

Isaiah 40:11

*Why do you complain, Jacob? Why do you say, Israel, "My way
is hidden from the Lord; my cause is disregarded by my God"? Do
you not know? Have you not heard? The Lord is the everlasting
God, the Creator of the ends of the earth. He will not grow tired
or weary, and his understanding no one can fathom.*

Isaiah 40:27–28

He gives strength to the weary and increases the power of the weak. Even youths grow tired and weary, and young men stumble and fall; but those who hope in the LORD will renew their strength. They will soar on wings like eagles; they will run and not grow weary, they will walk and not be faint.

Isaiah 40:29–31

The Lord Is Our Protector

Parents can be pretty intense when it comes to protecting their kids.

When children are tiny, it is all about babyproofing—setting up gates in front of stairs, putting guards on sharp corners, and locking cabinets filled with cleaning supplies.

Then the children get a little older, and parents frantically say a lot of the same phrases over and over: "Look both ways before you cross the street!" "Do you have your coat?" "Don't talk to strangers!"

A few more years pass, and moms and dads find themselves having hard conversations about texting and driving, safe dating, and on and on and on . . .

I am not sure a parent ever stops being concerned about a child's safety.

Have you ever thought about the truth that your heavenly Father wants to keep you, His child, safe too? Matthew 2 tells us about just such a time. Jesus was still young, probably a toddler, when His earthly father, Joseph, received an urgent warning from God in a dream.

"Get up," he said, "take the child and his mother and escape to Egypt. Stay there until I tell you, for Herod is going to search for the child to kill him" (vv. 13–14).

I wonder how Joseph felt when those urgent words interrupted his dreams. The angel's appearance—and message—must have been terrifying!

Jesus' very life depended on Joseph's willingness to listen and obey, and Joseph did not hesitate. Matthew 2:14 tells us he got up and took his family to safety that very night.

Just as Joseph loved and protected his son, God loves you and wants to keep you safe. He might speak to you urgently in a dream as He spoke to Joseph, but more often He speaks gently and softly.

One of the greatest gifts of spending time in quiet listening to God is getting to know His voice. Being able to recognize it opens the way for Him to speak into our lives and keep us from harm. Sometimes He will keep us from physical harm, but He seeks to keep us safe in so many other ways as well.

As a loving Father, He might warn us away from a toxic relationship or hold up a stop sign concerning a major life change. But one of the beautiful things about our Savior is that He also cares about the small things in our lives, about the habits that harm us and the old wounds that make us vulnerable.

When I was young, I didn't always go along with my mother's attempts to protect me. Now that I am older, I hope I am wiser. I want to follow Joseph's example by listening closely to my loving Father's words of protection in my life.

Like Joseph, may we never hesitate to obey!

> *Today I will listen for the Lord's voice and trust that He is watching over me.*

～ Five Minutes in the Word ～

The Lord is faithful, and he will strengthen you and protect you from the evil one.

2 Thessalonians 3:3

The sun will not harm you by day, nor the moon by night.

Psalm 121:6

If you say, "The LORD is my refuge," and you make
the Most High your dwelling, no harm will overtake
you, no disaster will come near your tent.

Psalm 91:9–10

The LORD will keep you from all
harm—he will watch over your life.

Psalm 121:7

The waywardness of the simple will kill them, and the
complacency of fools will destroy them; but whoever listens to
me will live in safety and be at ease, without fear of harm.

Proverbs 1:32–33

How He Longs for You

It is truly one of the most heartbreaking moments in all of Scripture.

In Matthew 23:37, we see Jesus' heart for Israel, His wandering people: "Jerusalem, Jerusalem, you who kill the prophets and stone those sent to you, how often I have longed to gather your children together, as a hen gathers her chicks under her wings, and you were not willing."

Jesus spoke these words to the Jews, but His divine words tell us a lot about the heart of God for all His people. Our heavenly Father longs for relationship with His children. He longs to protect them, to be near them, to hold them close to His heart.

Maybe you find that thought surprising, but we can find a lot of evidence in Scripture that God desires an intimate relationship with us. Way back in the garden, before God banished Adam and Eve from Eden, He made a promise that He would find a way to bring His children back home.

It would take centuries for that rescue story to play out. Battles would be waged and kingdoms would rise and fall, all as part of that rescue plan, all leading up to the birth of the Messiah.

And when that Messiah came, He loved to tell stories about God's longing heart. Jesus compared God and His lost children to a woman who searched for her precious lost coin, and to a shepherd who was so desperate to find one wayward sheep that he left all the other sheep to search for it and bring it home (Luke 15:1–10).

Finally, Jesus said, God's longing for His lost children was like a father who had lost his son, a father who would never give up and who would give absolutely anything to have his boy come home (vv. 11–32).

What about you? Have you wandered far away from home? Or perhaps you just need to hear your Father say those sweet words one more time:

"Oh, how I long to gather you near . . ."

> *You don't have to clean yourself up to come home to your Father. Just come.*

✎ Five Minutes in the Word ✎

"'My son,' the father said, 'you are always with me, and everything I have is yours. But we had to celebrate and be glad, because this brother of yours was dead and is alive again; he was lost and is found.'"

Luke 15:31–32

"I tell you that in the same way there will be more rejoicing in heaven over one sinner who repents than over ninety-nine righteous persons who do not need to repent."

Luke 15:7

"The Son of Man came to seek and to save the lost."

Luke 19:10

"I have swept away your offenses like a cloud, your sins like the morning mist. Return to me, for I have redeemed you."

Isaiah 44:22

"My sheep listen to my voice; I know them, and they follow me. I give them eternal life, and they shall never perish; no one will snatch them out of my hand."

John 10:27–28

Ears That Hear Him

Have you ever received news that broke your heart and took your breath away? In a moment like that, when God's promises don't seem to line up with your circumstances, it's easy to wonder where He is in the midst of your pain.

Those are the times we most need to get alone with God so we can try to get His perspective on things. We need to have ears to hear our heavenly Father when overwhelming problems surround us.

It was on February 7, 1938, that German pastor Martin Niemöller needed to hear from God in just this way. That morning Martin was led from his prison cell to the courtroom for his trial. His crime was daring to speak against Adolf Hitler.

Martin had been so courageous in the weeks and months leading up to that day, but as he began the long walk toward judgment, he found himself overcome with fear for himself and the people he loved.

Martin needed to hear from God.

The guard who led him along the passageway seemed cold as stone, but after a moment Martin began to hear a soft whispering. At first Martin wasn't sure what he was hearing, but as he listened more carefully, he realized it was the guard's voice. God's message to Martin was being delivered through the unlikeliest of messengers: a soldier of the Third Reich. He was whispering words from Proverbs that brought great comfort and courage to Martin's soul: "The name of the LORD is a strong tower; the righteous runs into it and is safe" (Proverbs 18:10 NASB).[1]

Are you, like Martin, overwhelmed by your circumstances today? Do you find yourself turning your situation over and over in your mind, desperate for a solution, then feeling knocked down by a fresh wave of fear?

Go to your heavenly Father. He knows what you are up against. Spend some time with Him so that He can fine-tune your hearing and remind you of who He is and what you mean to Him.

Perhaps there in the quiet you too will hear the gentle words Martin heard as he walked alone through one of the darkest moments in his life and in all of history: "The name of the LORD is a strong tower; the righteous runs into it and is safe."

> *Today, Lord, enable me to hear*
> *Your voice above every other.*

⊱ Five Minutes in the Word ⊰

He leads me beside quiet waters, he refreshes my soul. He guides me along the right paths for his name's sake. Even though I walk through the darkest valley, I will fear no evil, for you are with me; your rod and your staff, they comfort me.

Psalm 23:2–4

Strengthen the feeble hands, steady the knees that give way; say to those with fearful hearts, "Be strong, do not fear; your God will come, he will come with vengeance; with divine retribution he will come to save you."

Isaiah 35:3–4

"Do not fear, for I am with you; do not be dismayed,
for I am your God. I will strengthen you and help you; I
will uphold you with my righteous right hand."

Isaiah 41:10

Surely he will save you from the fowler's
snare and from the deadly pestilence.

Psalm 91:3

Fear of man will prove to be a snare, but
whoever trusts in the Lord is kept safe.

Proverbs 29:25

Rerouting

Sometimes I get the feeling my GPS is getting a little cross with me. She gives me directions, and I am pretty sure I'm following them. Then the next thing I know, she is correcting me.

"Rerouting," she says.

The first time she sounds remarkably polite and patient. And the second time too.

But the third time? The fourth? Perhaps I am imagining it, but I think she just called me something that could not be mistaken for a compliment under her breath!

Sometimes we think we are on the right path, *exactly* where God wants us to be, and then to our surprise, He interrupts us: "Rerouting . . ."

Peter had one of those moments in Acts 10. As a faithful Jew, he had learned about God's law throughout his whole life. What is more, everything we can gather about Peter from Scripture reveals a man who was serious about living in total obedience to that law. We find him in the synagogue and observing all the required feasts. Peter must have been pretty sure he was on the right path in life.

Then God completely rerouted him.

Scripture tells us that one day when Peter was praying on a rooftop, God came to him in a vision. He showed Peter a variety of animals that, according to Jewish law, were unclean to eat—and commanded him to eat them!

Peter was horrified. "Surely not, Lord! . . . I have never eaten anything impure or unclean" (Acts 10:14).

God was insistent, telling Peter that he shouldn't call anything He had made "unclean." And His message was really about much more than eating guidelines. God wanted Peter to know that since Jesus had redeemed all creation, the old divisions of Jews and non-Jews no longer applied. God was drawing *all* people to Himself. It was time for everyone to come home!

Did you notice what Peter was doing when he received this important change of direction for his life? He was taking time to be alone with God.

God is rarely as intrusive as our GPS. He waits for us in the stillness. It is often there that His loving voice surprises us with a new direction for our lives. I don't want to miss out on that, do you? Let's open our hearts for His rerouting today!

> *In the stillness we will hear God's voice saying, "This is the way!"*

⮞ Five Minutes in the Word ⮜

The LORD went before them by day in a pillar of cloud to lead the way, and by night in a pillar of fire to give them light, so as to go by day and night. He did not take away the pillar of cloud by day or the pillar of fire by night from before the people.

Exodus 13:21–22 NKJV

[Stephen] said, "Brethren and fathers, listen: The God of glory appeared to our father Abraham when he was in Mesopotamia, before he dwelt in Haran, and said to him, 'Get out of your country and from your relatives, and come to a land that I will show you.'"

Acts 7:2–3 NKJV

"I will instruct you and teach you in the way you should go; I will guide you with My eye."

Psalm 32:8 NKJV

Cause me to hear Your lovingkindness in the morning, for in You do I trust; cause me to know the way in which I should walk, for I lift up my soul to You.

Psalm 143:8 NKJV

Thus says the LORD, your Redeemer, the Holy One of Israel: "I am the LORD your God, who teaches you to profit, who leads you by the way you should go."

Isaiah 48:17 NKJV

The 34th Miner

Jorge Galleguillos never slowed his work deep beneath the surface of the earth as the mine creaked and cracked all around him. But at one point he looked up to see what looked like a white butterfly fluttering diagonally toward the cavern floor—just moments before steel buckled and snapped, and stone crashed down with a deafening roar.

That image, the wisp of delicate white, stuck with Jorge. How could he forget it? In his culture, the appearance of a white animal meant God was very near.

The nearness of God was indeed the light in the blackest midnight for Jorge and the other miners as they prayerfully awaited rescue. When the miracle of that moment dawned at last, sixty-nine unbelievable days later, the thirty-three men ascended the mine one by one with a common conviction: a thirty-fourth Miner had been with them beneath the mountain of rock, the Miner who holds the universe in the palm of His hands.[2]

The Chilean miners could truly, joyfully proclaim with the psalmist, "If I go up to the heavens, you are there; if I make my bed in the depths, you are there" (Psalm 139:8).

God's presence with us is a priceless gift! In Numbers 6, when God instructed the new priests how to bless the Israelites, He didn't tell them to bless Israel with riches and success or even security. He knew that the greatest blessing His people could ever receive was the gift of *His presence*.

Listen: "The LORD bless you and keep you; the LORD make his face shine on you and be gracious to you; the LORD turn his face toward you and give you peace" (vv. 24–26).

Stop for a moment and read that priestly blessing again, this time slowly. Do you feel that tugging? That gentle longing in your heart?

Your heart belongs in the presence of your loving God. He stands ready to turn His face toward you and to be gracious to you. And He longs to give you His peace.

> *In the darkest night, God is our ever-present Light!*

༄ Five Minutes in the Word ༅

In the shelter of your presence you hide them from all human intrigues;
you keep them safe in your dwelling from accusing tongues.

Psalm 31:20

Blessed are those who have learned to acclaim you,
who walk in the light of your presence, LORD.

Psalm 89:15

Where can I go from your Spirit? Where can I flee from your presence?

Psalm 139:7

The LORD gives strength to his people; the LORD
blesses his people with peace.

Psalm 29:11

If I say, "Surely the darkness will hide me and the light become
night around me," even the darkness will not be dark to you; the
night will shine like the day, for darkness is as light to you.

Psalm 139:11–12

Does God Care When
I Am Hurting?

I could see the pain in her eyes before she spoke a single word. I had just finished speaking at a conference on the East Coast, and she had waited off to one side until I finished signing books and meeting other women. She looked me straight in the eyes and paused before she said, "I don't believe what you shared from the stage today."

"Thank you for being honest with me," I said. "What did you disagree with?"

"You said that God is a loving Father who cares for us," she replied.

"I believe that with everything in me," I told her. "Why do you struggle to believe that God loves you?"

Again, a pause. "Because I have buried two sons."

I held her as tears coursed down her face and her fragile frame shook.

Her question is an age-old one: "My God, do You care when I am hurting?"

I think Mary and Martha were wondering the same thing when their brother, Lazarus, died. You see, these sisters had seen Jesus do so many amazing things that when Lazarus became ill, they knew that all they needed to do was get word to Jesus and their brother would be healed. Jesus could do it!

And He could have.

But . . . He didn't.

John 11:5–6 tells us that Jesus "loved Martha and her sister and Lazarus," but when He received the news that Lazarus was sick, Jesus delayed going to him for "two more days." By the time Jesus arrived in Bethany, Lazarus was already in the tomb, and Mary and Martha were in mourning.

It is easy to understand why Martha and Mary might have wondered whether Jesus cared that they were hurting. In fact, Martha's first words to Jesus were, "If you had been here, my brother would not have died" (v. 21).

What Martha and Mary did not know was that Jesus delayed going to them so that He might demonstrate God's power and glory. Jesus had a plan that was far more wonderful than just healing Lazarus. *He was going to raise Lazarus from the dead!*

There is something beautiful recorded for us in verses 33 through 35 that we must not miss. When Jesus saw the sisters and all of Lazarus's friends mourning, He Himself broke down and wept.

His heart was broken over their grief!

I don't know what you are facing right now, but I know that God loves you and wants to comfort you in your pain. Will you let Him in? Talk to Him about your pain. He is very near.

Jesus truly is Emmanuel, "God with us."

⁓⌀ Five Minutes in the Word ⌀⁓

My eyes are dim with grief. I call to you, LORD,
every day; I spread out my hands to you.

Psalm 88:9

You, God, see the trouble of the afflicted; you consider their
grief and take it in hand. The victims commit themselves
to you; you are the helper of the fatherless.

Psalm 10:14

The LORD is close to the brokenhearted and

saves those who are crushed in spirit.

Psalm 34:18

The LORD builds up Jerusalem; he gathers the exiles of Israel.

He heals the brokenhearted and binds up their wounds.

Psalm 147:2–3

"He will wipe every tear from their eyes. There will

be no more death or mourning or crying or pain,

for the old order of things has passed away."

Revelation 21:4

Object Lessons

Back before Sunday school lessons on DVDs and choreographed kids' worship times was the magic of flannel boards. Remember those? Today's children might find the soft flannel figures of Bible characters a bit lame, but there was a time when they were the highlight of the Sunday school lesson.

Jesus didn't use video lessons or flannel boards in His teaching, but He still taught powerful truths through object lessons, often using an aspect of His creation to illuminate a spiritual truth.

Matthew 6, for instance, tells of a moment when Jesus wanted to assure His followers that there was no need to worry about whether their daily needs would be met. To illustrate that truth, Jesus turned to nature to show them God's faithfulness.

"Look at the birds of the air; for they neither sow nor reap nor gather into barns; yet your heavenly Father feeds them. Are you not of more value than they? . . . So why do you worry about clothing? Consider the lilies of the field, how they grow: they neither toil nor spin" (vv. 26, 28 NKJV).

Jesus was telling His followers to look around and see that God was providing for all He had made—and providing abundantly. He wanted to assure them that if God took such good care of birds and lilies, He would certainly take care of them.

It is a truth God is still teaching through His creation more than two thousand years later—if only we are willing to stop and tune in to what He is saying. And that's a good thing because, if you are like me, this is a truth you need to hear over and over again.

Do you ever worry about having what you need, what your loved ones need? Do you worry about the bottom line of your bank account? Perhaps you've been tossing and turning in middle-of-the-night darkness, your chest tight, wondering how you will pay the bills.

Take some time today to look out your window and ask God to give you eyes to see how faithful He is to His creation. Then lay before His throne every one of your needs in the confidence that you are infinitely more valuable to Him than the birds of the air or the flowers of the fields.

Look at the birds . . .

Consider the lilies . . .

If He cares for them, He will care for you too.

> *Cast your cares on*
> *Him . . . He cares for you.*

‍ Five Minutes in the Word ‍

All creatures look to you to give them their food at the proper
time. When you give it to them, they gather it up; when you
open your hand, they are satisfied with good things.

Psalm 104:27–28

The righteous will flourish like a palm tree, they will grow like
a cedar of Lebanon; planted in the house of the LORD, they will
flourish in the courts of our God. They will still bear fruit in old
age, they will stay fresh and green, proclaiming, "The LORD is
upright; he is my Rock, and there is no wickedness in him."

Psalm 92:12–15

Let them give thanks to the LORD for his unfailing love
and his wonderful deeds for mankind, for he satisfies
the thirsty and fills the hungry with good things.

Psalm 107:8–9

Fear the LORD, you his holy people, for
those who fear him lack nothing.

Psalm 34:9

The LORD makes firm the steps of the one who delights
in him; though he may stumble, he will not fall, for
the LORD upholds him with his hand. I was young
and now I am old, yet I have never seen the righteous
forsaken or their children begging bread.

Psalm 37:23–25

Where Are You?

Have you seen the movie *Cast Away*? The movie tells the story of an ordinary man who found himself alone on an island after an airplane crash. In order to survive he learned to build shelter, find food, and even start a fire without a match. One of his most interesting survival techniques was turning a volleyball, which had washed onto shore, into a companion. After grabbing the ball with a bloody hand, he realized the imprint looked remarkably like a face. He added eyes, a nose, and a mouth, and noticing the brand, named it "Wilson."[3]

The point is this: we need companionship just as much as we need food, clothing, and shelter.

You have probably thought about your need for human companionship, but have you ever realized how desperately your spirit longs for one-on-one time with God?

The creation story in Genesis reveals the important truth that we were made to know and love God and to be known and loved by Him.

When we turn back the pages of history to the moment just after sin entered the world, we find a scene of broken beauty as God showed up in the garden. He had come to walk in the cool of the day with His children, with His friends, with Adam and Eve.

But a terrible thing had happened.

The serpent had told a lie . . .

God's children had disobeyed Him . . .

Now they were in hiding . . .

And it would take thousands of years and the sacrifice of a sinless Savior to make things right again.

In the moment just before Adam and Eve's sin was revealed, we see the God of the universe surveying the garden, looking for His precious children, only to find they were hiding from Him. Then we hear His heartbreaking cry, "Where are you?" (Genesis 3:9). It's not that God didn't know where Adam and Eve were; He just didn't want them to hide from Him. He had created them so He could love them.

God is calling for you today. He loves you. He longs to spend time with you so He can show you just how much He loves you. Find a quiet place and open your heart to Him. Your spirit needs His gentle touch as much as your body needs food, clothing, and shelter.

You were created to be loved by God.

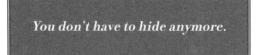

You don't have to hide anymore.

‹⁓ Five Minutes in the Word ⁓›

I keep asking that the God of our Lord Jesus Christ, the
glorious Father, may give you the Spirit of wisdom and
revelation, so that you may know him better.

Ephesians 1:17

We know also that the Son of God has come and has given us
understanding, so that we may know him who is true.

1 John 5:20

I want to know Christ—yes, to know the power of his resurrection
and participation in his sufferings, becoming like him in his death,
and so, somehow, attaining to the resurrection from the dead.

Philippians 3:10–11

The Lord appeared to us in the past, saying: "I have loved you with
an everlasting love; I have drawn you with unfailing kindness."

Jeremiah 31:3

He brought me to the banqueting house, and his banner over me was love.

Song of Solomon 2:4 NKJV

Are You Listening?

My darling husband, Barry, suffers from a hearing disorder that makes me crazy. He has a severe case of selective listening. Consider this conversation from a few nights ago.

"I think it would look nice if we repainted the living room," I said.

"Hmm, good idea," he replied.

"I'm thinking we could either paint it a light yellow to give a warm glow or even a pale teal to pick up that color in the rug."

"True," he responded.

"But I think the teal might be a little cold," I said. "What do you think?"

"About what?"

"The living room."

"What about the living room?"

My husband's difficulty in this area is a family joke,

but there are times when you need to know you're being heard.

And there are times when you need to be listening carefully.

Have you ever found yourself trying to share your heart with someone who wasn't really listening? How did that make you feel? I bet that at the end of the conversation you felt that he or she didn't really care about you . . . perhaps didn't even care to know you.

God wants us to listen to Him, to know Him. Throughout Scripture we find God speaking as He reveals Himself to people. First, we see God speak the world into existence, then talk with the first man and woman (Genesis 1; 2:16). He spoke through His law and through His prophets (Exodus 24:12; Deuteronomy 18:18).

In the New Testament, things really got exciting as God began to speak through His Son, Jesus, and then through the Holy Spirit (John 1:1; 14:26).

God is still revealing Himself to us today. He is still speaking! We are His children, and He loves us. *He wants to be known by us.*

When I stop to think that the eternal, almighty Creator

wants me to know Him, I just can't help but get excited. What an amazing gift!

But how can we truly know God if we fail to make the time and space to listen to Him?

May we take the time today to give Him our full attention, rest in His sweet presence, and listen. May we learn His voice so we can know Him more.

Speak, Lord, for Your servant is listening.

⊱ᴄᴏ Five Minutes in the Word ᴈᴏ⊰

Faith comes by hearing, and hearing by the word of God.
Romans 10:17 NKJV

In the past God spoke to our ancestors through the prophets
at many times and in various ways, but in these last days he
has spoken to us by his Son, whom he appointed heir of all
things, and through whom also he made the universe.

Hebrews 1:1–2

The Word became flesh and made his dwelling among us.
We have seen his glory, the glory of the one and only Son,
who came from the Father, full of grace and truth.

John 1:14

We are in him who is true by being in his Son Jesus
Christ. He is the true God and eternal life.

1 John 5:20

"I am the good shepherd; I know my sheep and my sheep know
me—just as the Father knows me and I know the Father—and I
lay down my life for the sheep. . . . My sheep listen to my voice; I
know them, and they follow me. I give them eternal life, and they
shall never perish; no one will snatch them out of my hand."

John 10:14–15, 27–28

Love Changes Things

I'm not a good Wemmick," Punchinello would say.

Punchinello had heard one too many critical comments, taken one too many hits to the heart. He had gotten back up time and again, but eventually he could no longer shake off the lies about his self-worth. He started to believe them.

In Max Lucado's brilliant children's book *You Are Special*, Punchinello and the other wooden people called Wemmicks had an unusual custom. Each one of them carried around two boxes of stickers to give their fellow Wemmicks: a box of gold stars and a box of gray dots. If a Wemmick did something impressive, his neighbor might give him a gold star. If he made a mistake, he received a dreaded gray dot. After a while, a Wemmick might find himself receiving a disapproving gray dot simply because he already had so many. That's what happened to Punchinello. And all of those gray dots had taken their toll on him.

But then he met Lucia, a Wemmick who was completely sticker-free! Lucia explained to Punchinello the secret of her freedom: she simply spent time with Eli, the Woodcarver, every day.

The next morning Punchinello walked up the hill to visit Eli. He was nervous about the visit because he was so ashamed of his dots, but it turned out Eli didn't care.

"I think you are pretty special," Eli explained, "because you are mine."[4]

I don't know about you, but I understand Punchinello's struggle. I too have longed for the approval of others . . . and have found myself unsure and wounded after one too many criticisms has been lobbed my way. Perhaps some people are so naturally resilient and self-assured that they can just brush it all off, but I'm not one of them. I need the voice of One more powerful. Like Punchinello, I need time with my Maker. I need to hear Him say, "You are special because you belong to Me."

Sometimes the relentless assault of our fallen world can leave us numb, weary, and heartsore. That's when we need to be reminded again just how much God loves us. After all, in His presence everything changes. Death is raised to life. Sorrow is turned to joy. And all of our brokenness and insecurities are lost when He shows us the truth about who we really are.

Love, you see, changes things.

Have you, like Punchinello, received one too many gray dots this week? Rest your heart in the presence of your Maker. Let Him remind you just how much He loves you—and let Him remove every gray dot!

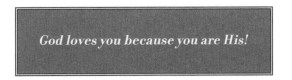

God loves you because you are His!

⟿ Five Minutes in the Word ⟿

We have thought, O God, on Your
lovingkindness, in the midst of Your temple.
Psalm 48:9 NKJV

I will be glad and rejoice in your love, for you saw
my affliction and knew the anguish of my soul.
Psalm 31:7

He has given me a new song to sing, a hymn of praise to our God.
Many will see what he has done and be amazed. They will put
their trust in the LORD. Oh, the joys of those who trust the LORD, who
have no confidence in the proud or in those who worship idols. . . .
Let your unfailing love and faithfulness always protect me.

Psalm 40:3–4, 11 NLT

Because your love is better than
life, my lips will glorify you.

Psalm 63:3

Your love, LORD, reaches to the heavens,
your faithfulness to the skies.

Psalm 36:5

Does God See Me?

The letters arrived in Jesse's mailbox a couple of times each week. They were typed in a feminine font on blue or pink paper with a woman's name signed at the bottom: "Pamela." Each night, exhausted and painfully lonely, Jesse closed the door to his room and spread the pages of the letters across his bed. Jesse had never been in a relationship before, but with Pamela, he finally felt like he mattered to someone.

And Pamela was happy to keep writing to him . . . for a small fee.

Several years and thousands of dollars later, Jesse discovered that Pamela was, in fact, a scam artist named Don Lowry. Yet Jesse found it difficult to completely discard all that Pamela had meant to him. She had made him believe that there was "someone out there looking out for him."[5]

My heart breaks for lonely people like Jesse. When I think about him, Leah from the Old Testament comes to mind. Leah's name meant "weary, tired," but I sometimes wonder if Leah was more than weary and tired.[6] I wonder if she felt . . . invisible.

You see, Genesis 29 paints a painful picture of her: verse 17 contrasts Leah's "weak eyes" with her younger sister, Rachel, who "had a lovely figure and was beautiful." Then we learn that a young man named Jacob was in love with Rachel and wanted to marry her, but when the wedding night arrived, the girls' father tricked Jacob into marrying Leah instead! When Jacob realized he had married Leah, his first words to his father-in-law were, "What is this you have done to me?" (v. 25). Poor Leah! Can you imagine?

Sadly, Leah's circumstances got worse. When she and Jacob had been married only one week, he married Rachel too. From that time on, Leah had to live in the shadow of their love. She was the ultimate third wheel.

But Leah, the invisible girl, wasn't invisible to everyone. *God* saw her. He saw her loneliness, rejection, and broken heart, and He cared deeply about her. Listen to these remarkable words: "When the LORD saw that Leah was not loved, he enabled her to conceive, but Rachel remained childless. Leah became pregnant and gave birth to a son. She named him Reuben, for she said, 'It is because the LORD has seen my misery'" (vv. 31–32).

For everyone who has ever felt invisible, or wondered if anyone in the world noticed her or cared about her broken heart, this short passage holds an ocean of hope.

Our God sees. He cares when we are hurt and lonely.

So come . . .

Rest in Him today . . .

And let His great love restore your soul.

> *He is the God who sees you . . . and loves you.*

⋙ Five Minutes in the Word ⋘

She gave this name to the LORD who spoke to her: "You are the God who sees me," for she said, "I have now seen the One who sees me."

Genesis 16:13

You see the trouble and grief they cause. You take note of it and punish them. The helpless put their trust in you. You defend the orphans.

Psalm 10:14 NLT

From heaven the Lord looks down and sees all mankind;
from his dwelling place he watches all who live on earth.

Psalm 33:13–14

For the eyes of the Lord range throughout the earth to
strengthen those whose hearts are fully committed to him.

2 Chronicles 16:9

But the eyes of the Lord are on those who fear him,
on those whose hope is in his unfailing love, to deliver
them from death and keep them alive in famine.

Psalm 33:18–19

The Great Physician

I didn't think my mom would notice. After all, it was just a few coins from her purse. And it wasn't for cigarettes or beer. It was so I could join my friends in pursuing the latest fad . . . peapods.

I don't remember now who started this craze, but it caught on quickly. We would each buy a big bag of peas, still in their pods, and then sit on the hill behind our homes and eat them, raw. On this particular night I had no allowance left, and rather than stay home, I decided to steal a few coins from my mother's purse.

Just before bedtime Mom asked my sister, my brother, and me if we knew where the coins in her purse were as she had been saving them for something. I still remember the sickening feeling as I lied to my mom and told her I had no idea. I tried to go to sleep . . . but I couldn't shake my shame. My sin had caused a barrier in my heart not only between my mom and me but also between God and me. It was like trying to ignore a big, bleeding wound.

I had a *sin wound*, and I needed a Healer.

Seeing sin as a wound is a subtle shift, but a significant one. If that night I had believed, as I do now, that Jesus sees our sin not as a failure to condemn but as a wound to heal, I would have been quicker to confess!

In Jeremiah 6, God confronted Israel for breaking their covenant with Him. They had done this by oppressing the weak. Even worse, God's prophets had tried to cover Israel's offense. God said this of the prophets: "They dress the wound of my people as though it were not serious. 'Peace, peace,' they say, when there is no peace" (v. 14).

Israel's sin was a wound, a spiritual one.

When we sin, we wound the people around us, but we also wound our own souls that were made in the image of God.

So now, when I enter into God's presence, I find myself eager to confess. I know He loves me and wants to heal the sin wound in me. I don't need to feel ashamed when I am in the presence of my gracious and kind Great Physician.

Come into His presence and lay your sin wound at His feet. Healing awaits you.

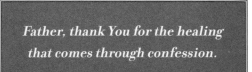

Father, thank You for the healing
that comes through confession.

"It is not the healthy who need a doctor, but the sick.
I have not come to call the righteous, but sinners."
Mark 2:17

I acknowledged my sin to you and did not cover up my
iniquity. I said, "I will confess my transgressions to
the Lord." And you forgave the guilt of my sin.
Psalm 32:5

Since we have these promises, dear friends, let us purify
ourselves from everything that contaminates body and
spirit, perfecting holiness out of reverence for God.
2 Corinthians 7:1

Cleanse me with hyssop, and I will be clean;
wash me, and I will be whiter than snow.
Psalm 51:7

Let us draw near to God with a sincere heart and with the full assurance
that faith brings, having our hearts sprinkled to cleanse us from a
guilty conscience and having our bodies washed with pure water.
Hebrews 10:22

Does God Love Me?

Everything was about to change.

For three years, Jesus had walked beside His disciples. He had taught them God's truth, lived out God's love, done amazing miracles to demonstrate God's power, and told them about God's salvation plan. As they walked, He taught, pointing out practical lessons along the way.

And now they were walking again and He was teaching again, but this time it was different because Jesus' time with His disciples was short and *everything was about to change.*

Jesus knew the last moments were ticking away before His return to His Father. As He anticipated making the ultimate sacrifice of His very life, a sacrifice that would rend the veil between God and humanity forever, He began His last lessons: "Greater love has no one than this: to lay down one's life for one's friends" (John 15:13).

I am filled with wonder that out of all the ways Jesus

could have spent His precious last hours on earth, He chose to spend more time talking to His followers about how much He and the Father loved them and how He wanted them to love one another.

Jesus loves you and me. This is the same Jesus who was there when the first sunrise broke through the darkness of the new world. He placed the stars in the sky and called each one by name. He could see into the future as every kingdom of this world would rise and fall. He knew that His disciples would suffer for His name and the words of strength each of them would need to endure those trials.

And what better source of strength than reassurance of His great love?

Jesus chose to spend His precious final moments telling His followers how much He loves all of us . . . meaning *you and me.*

Do you wonder sometimes whether God loves you? Do you ask yourself how it could possibly be true? Like a child, do you want to ask Him, "How much? How much do you love me?"

Close your eyes . . . still your heart . . . and hear Him as He says, "This is the very best way to love. Put your life on the line for your friends. You are my friends" (John 15:13 THE MESSAGE).

He loved you all the way to the cross . . .

He loves you now, in this very moment . . .

And He will love you all the way home to heaven!

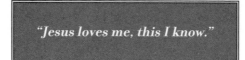

"Jesus loves me, this I know."

⊱ Five Minutes in the Word ⊰

*This is love: not that we loved God, but that he loved us
and sent his Son as an atoning sacrifice for our sins.*

1 John 4:10

*"For God so loved the world that he gave his one and only Son, that
whoever believes in him shall not perish but have eternal life."*

John 3:16

*"A new command I give you: Love one another. As I
have loved you, so you must love one another."*

John 13:34

"As the Father has loved me, so have I loved you. Now remain in my love."

John 15:9

*As God's chosen people, holy and dearly loved, clothe yourselves
with compassion, kindness, humility, gentleness and patience.*

Colossians 3:12

Permission to
Stop Pretending

In 1968, Apollo 8 astronaut William Anders shook the watching world to its core. The mission to orbit the moon was being televised, and millions were tuned in for a glimpse of space. At one point Anders noticed something the three astronauts hadn't seen because of the spacecraft's angle: "Oh . . . look at that picture over there. There's the Earth coming up. Wow, is that pretty!"[7]

And there it was . . . a breathtaking white and blue half sphere suspended against the infinite blackness of space. In the photo later named "Earthrise," the public saw planet Earth from space for the first time.[8] I was only twelve years old, and I'll never forget it. Suddenly, we all seemed smaller; the Earth, more fragile yet profoundly beautiful; and our existence, more miraculous than ever before.

I think that glimpse of the universe's vastness gives us

a small taste of what it's like to glimpse the holiness of God and the glory of His presence. As we consider His infinite power—evident in the force of earthquakes, the miracle of a baby, and the intricacy of a rose—we are reminded of our smallness.

Humility before God doesn't come easily for us. Israel certainly struggled with it. In the final chapter of Isaiah, God described the type of person He looks on with favor. It isn't the most talented person or most successful. It is the one who has looked long and hard at her almighty, holy Creator and has seen herself accurately in comparison.

"This is what the LORD says: 'Heaven is my throne, and the earth is my footstool. . . . Has not my hand made all these things, and so they came into being?' declares the LORD. 'These are the ones I look on with favor: those who are humble and contrite in spirit, and who tremble at my word'" (Isaiah 66:1–2).

Here, the word *humble* can also be translated "lame." The implication? This person who catches God's attention has glimpsed His holiness and has a keen awareness of the crippling effect of sin in her life, and the contrast has humbled her.[9]

But why is humility so important to paving the way to hearing from God?

Humility allows us to quit pretending we have it all together, have all the answers, or are in need of nothing. It clears the way for us to simply . . . receive.

What a relief, right? How wonderful would it be to just let down your guard in the presence of Perfect Love and come just as you are! When you do, you will find the Shepherd of your soul waiting there for you.

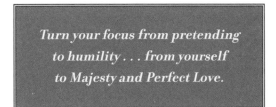

Turn your focus from pretending to humility . . . from yourself to Majesty and Perfect Love.

⟿ Five Minutes in the Word ⟾

You save the humble, but your eyes are on the haughty to bring them low. You, LORD, are my lamp; the LORD turns my darkness into light.

2 Samuel 22:28–29

He guides the humble in what is
right and teaches them his way.

Psalm 25:9

God opposes the proud but
shows favor to the humble.

James 4:6

Do not be like the horse or the mule, which have
no understanding but must be controlled by
bit and bridle or they will not come to you.

Psalm 32:9

Be completely humble and gentle;
be patient, bearing with one another in love.

Ephesians 4:2

Like a Child

I may have told you that I have one child, but that head count is quite inaccurate. Barry and I have, in fact, one son and three small, furry, opinionated dogs. If you're not a dog person, you may find it hard to grasp that having one child and three dogs is, in fact, like having four children.

Take Belle, our oldest dog, for example. She believes that everyone on television is actually in our living room, and she feels obliged to greet them accordingly.

Tink is entitlement on four legs. She knows that every self-respecting dog gets a treat for being gracious enough to eat her meal and will bark until the aforementioned treat is offered.

Maggie loves her toys and wants me to play with them and her for about twenty-five hours a day.

Children—furry or otherwise—look to Mom to take care of everything. They think Mom can solve any problem that arises. And Mom is never supposed to get tired, run out of patience, or just . . . blow it. Mom is supposed to be *limitless*. It is a cruel shock to a child on the day he or she realizes that Mom is, in fact, human.

But I love the confidence children have in their mothers. They fully believe their mothers will always be there, ready to address every need, like a never-ending fountain of personalized care and provision. I want to approach God with *that* kind of belief in Him!

Jesus told His disciples that if they wanted to enter the kingdom of God, they needed to first become like little children (Matthew 18:3–4).

How do we approach God "like a child"?

With confidence and trust . . .

With an attitude of dependence . . .

With a heart ready to receive . . .

With an unrelenting, never-give-up belief in His power *(I know You can meet my need!)*.

Mom may not be able to solve everything, but God can. In Him, we find a deep well for our thirsty souls. When we enter His presence with a childlike heart, we can say with the psalmist, "All my fountains are in you" (Psalm 87:7).

⁓ Five Minutes in the Word ⁓

*"Which of you, if your son asks for bread, will give him a stone? Or
if he asks for a fish, will give him a snake? If you, then, though you
are evil, know how to give good gifts to your children, how much more
will your Father in heaven give good gifts to those who ask him!"*

Matthew 7:9–11

*I have calmed and quieted myself, I am like a weaned child
with its mother; like a weaned child I am content. Israel,
put your hope in the LORD both now and forevermore.*

Psalm 131:2–3

*"This, then, is how you should pray: 'Our
Father in heaven, hallowed be your name.'"*

Matthew 6:9

*"Truly I tell you, anyone who will not receive the kingdom of God
like a little child will never enter it." And he took the children
in his arms, placed his hands on them and blessed them.*

Mark 10:15–16

"When you pray, do not keep on babbling like the pagans, for they think they will be heard because of their many words. Do not be like them, for your Father knows what you need before you ask him."

Matthew 6:7–8

The LORD is trustworthy in all he promises and faithful in all he does. The LORD upholds all who fall and lifts up all who are bowed down. The eyes of all look to you, and you give them their food at the proper time. You open your hand and satisfy the desires of every living thing.

Psalm 145:13–16

I Will Meditate on Your Word

Elias Howe was working nonstop on his new invention, the sewing machine, but no matter what he tried, the stitches turned out sloppy. He was so focused on the problem that one night he dreamed he had been kidnapped by a group of tribesmen and given twenty-four hours to finish his invention!

When his time was up in the dream, Elias still was unsuccessful. Right before the nightmare ended, lots of the tribesmen's spears were flying at him. But there was something strange about those spears: each one had a small hole near the tip.

When Elias awoke, he had the answer to the problem with the sewing machine. The stitches would neaten up if he put the eye of the needle near the tip. He had solved the problem while he slept![10]

Imagine what God would do in our hearts and minds if we were focused that intently on His Word! Meditating on it is one of the ways God speaks to us, and it's mentioned throughout Scripture. The first person we find meditating is Isaac, all the way back in Genesis 24:63.

And yet meditating on God's Word is a skill lost to many Christians today. Perhaps you've considered it, but felt a little intimidated or didn't know where to begin. Let me take some of the mystery out of it for you.

The word *meditate* simply means "to think intently and at length, as to spiritual purposes."[11] One simple way to meditate on Scripture is to write down or memorize a short passage, even one verse, and then find a quiet place where you can focus on it for a while. I always like to begin my time with a brief prayer: I ask the Holy Spirit to help me understand the verse and how He wants to apply it to my life. Then meditating is simply a matter of gently returning my mind to the verse each time it begins to wander. Slowly, the Holy Spirit works in me to help me understand the passage.

I also find it helpful to keep a journal and pen nearby to jot down what I've discovered. As a matter of fact, journaling Scripture—writing it out and then recording your observations—can be a form of scriptural meditation all its own.

It's important to just enjoy the process. Really let yourself slow down for a few minutes and wait for what God wants to show you. Who knows? Perhaps the fruit of your meditation will come to you in a dream as it did for Elias Howe! (If you are by chance trying to invent a way to remove all the calories from chocolate, I personally hope so.)

One thing I do know, God can't wait to talk with you.

I will still my heart to hear Your voice.

⮜ Five Minutes in the Word ⮞

Keep this Book of the Law always on your lips; meditate on it day and night, so that you may be careful to do everything written in it. Then you will be prosperous and successful.
Joshua 1:8

Within your temple, O God, we meditate on your unfailing love.
Psalm 48:9

I have more insight than all my teachers,

for I meditate on your statutes.

Psalm 119:99

My eyes stay open through the watches of the night,

that I may meditate on your promises.

Psalm 119:148

If any of you lacks wisdom, you should ask God, who gives
generously to all without finding fault, and it will be given to you.

James 1:5

O Love That Will
Not Let Me Go

I sat on the floor of my hospital room and wept. I'd spent so much of my life trying to be the perfect Christian woman and now, here I was, in a psychiatric ward, alone and afraid.

In time, I would come to understand the beast that is clinical depression and that there is help and hope, but at that moment I felt as if I had gone to hell. I rested my head on my knees and suddenly from somewhere, somewhere deep inside, the words of a hymn flooded over me:

> *O Love that will not let me go,*
> *I rest my weary soul in Thee;*
> *I give Thee back the life I owe,*
> *That in Thine ocean depths its flow*
> *May richer, fuller be.*

I had sung that hymn since I was a child in our little Baptist church on the west coast of Scotland, but that night, the words became an anchor for me when I was sinking fast.

I discovered some time later that a fellow Scot named George Matheson wrote those words in 1882 during a night of intense suffering in his soul. He could never have imagined the hope they would bring to me so many years later.

God still speaks through the great hymns of the church today! A. W. Tozer once remarked, "After the sacred Scriptures, the next best companion for the soul is a good hymnal."[12]

The hymns connect us to the body of Christ throughout the ages, to fellow believers in struggles and victories, as well as to the powerful truths about God they discovered in the process. Through the gift of music, these deep spiritual lessons are given to us in a way that we can easily receive and remember.

The music and the poetry open our hearts.

Could it be that God has refreshment for your soul between the covers of a hymnbook? Why not find one and keep it nearby for your quiet time with the Father? You just may find a fresh word from God in the worn pages of a much-loved hymnal.

⟡ Five Minutes in the Word ⟡

[Speak] to one another with psalms, hymns, and songs from the Spirit.
Sing and make music from your heart to the Lord, always giving thanks
to God the Father for everything, in the name of our Lord Jesus Christ.
Ephesians 5:19–20

Sing praises to God, sing praises; sing praises to our King, sing praises.
For God is the King of all the earth; sing to him a psalm of praise.
Psalm 47:6–7

Christ has become a servant of the Jews on behalf of God's
truth, so that the promises made to the patriarchs might be
confirmed and, moreover, that the Gentiles might glorify God
for his mercy. As it is written: "Therefore I will praise you
among the Gentiles; I will sing the praises of your name."
Romans 15:8–9

Praise the LORD. How good it is to sing praises to our
God, how pleasant and fitting to praise him!

Psalm 147:1

Let the message of Christ dwell among you richly as you teach and
admonish one another with all wisdom through psalms, hymns, and
songs from the Spirit, singing to God with gratitude in your hearts.

Colossians 3:16

Wait on the Lord

I was rewinding an old VHS tape to show Christian and his friends some footage from our trip to Scotland when he was two years old.

"This is taking forever," one of them said.

"Does this thing run on gas?" another asked.

I laughed at their horror of anything that takes longer than three seconds to load. We live in such a "now" culture, where everything is immediately available at the touch of a button or with a voice command.

Waiting. It isn't easy, especially when we are waiting on God, but Scripture is filled with the stories of men and women who experienced agonizing periods of waiting on the Lord.

Abram and Sarai waited twenty-five years for God to fulfill His promise that *someday* they would have a child. When Isaac was born, they were old enough to be great-grandparents!

The Israelites suffered for more than four hundred years in Egyptian slavery, waiting for God to deliver them from their cruel bondage.

After Samuel had anointed him king of Israel, David waited years to assume the throne that was rightfully his.

For three long days Jesus' followers waited for hope to break through their darkest despair as His battered body lay in the tomb.

Jesus rose from the dead and returned to the Father to prepare a home for us, and we who call Him Savior and Lord have been waiting more than two thousand years for Him to return.

The difficult work of waiting often seems to be part of our relationship with God. His timing is just different from ours. The apostle Peter wrote, "Do not forget this one thing, dear friends: With the Lord a day is like a thousand years, and a thousand years are like a day" (2 Peter 3:8).

What does this have to do with our quiet time with God? When I enter into that space with God, I often experience a period of waiting, and I think that comes with being human. Don't be discouraged if you struggle to quiet your mind or you feel as if your prayers are bouncing off the ceiling. Grant yourself the gift of relaxing into the wait. If you gently continue to turn your heart back to Him, simply waiting on Him, you will experience His presence.

And His presence will be worth the wait!

> *I choose to step into the quiet and wait for You.*

⁓⟲⟋ Five Minutes in the Word ⟍⟋⟋⟋

I wait for you; you will answer, Lord my God.

Psalm 38:15

Be strong and take heart, all you who hope in the LORD.

Psalm 31:24

*In the morning, LORD, you hear my voice; in the morning
I lay my requests before you and wait expectantly.*

Psalm 5:3

*Be still before the LORD and wait patiently for him; do not fret when
people succeed in their ways, when they carry out their wicked schemes*

Psalm 37:7

We wait in hope for the LORD; he is our help and our shield.

Psalm 33:20

Secret Weapon

The gates to the Japanese concentration camp swung open, allowing the newly liberated prisoners to walk free. Utterly broken, they slowly walked away from brutality so severe that they no longer had the strength even to lift their heads.

Except for one person.

Her face was still vibrant and alive.

The spirit of this woman, a missionary, had endured because she had a secret weapon: a contraband copy of the gospel of John. Each night, with her blanket pulled over her head, she risked death by reading a small passage by flashlight and memorizing it. Once she committed a page to memory, she sneaked it to the bathhouse and let water run on it until it dissolved down the drain. She ended up memorizing the entire gospel, and God's Word protected her mind and heart in an impossible situation.[13]

I pray you haven't suffered such harsh circumstances

and never will, but I hope you have experienced the power of God's Word in your life. So many times over the years God has spoken to me by bringing scripture to mind. Each time it happens, I am so thankful that I have spent time in His Word, reading and rereading certain passages until I have committed them to memory. I can only imagine how much it frustrates the Enemy when he thinks he has me discouraged . . . only to watch helplessly as the Holy Spirit reminds me of the words I need in order to stand strong in that moment!

I also treasure the comfort and strength God brings through memorized Scripture when I can't sleep and my heart is troubled. On many nights I have drifted off to sleep by going through the scriptures stored in my mind. Like the psalmist, I have found that when my "soul is weary with sorrow," God will "strengthen me according to [His] word" (Psalm 119:28).

One of the greatest gifts you can ever give yourself is to hide God's Word in your heart. He is forever speaking through His Word to bring comfort and strength to your soul.

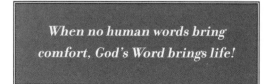

When no human words bring comfort, God's Word brings life!

～❦ Five Minutes in the Word ❦～

Your word is a lamp for my feet,
a light on my path.

Psalm 119:105

I have hidden your word in my heart
that I might not sin against you.

Psalm 119:11

The word of God is alive and active. Sharper than any double-
edged sword, it penetrates even to dividing soul and spirit, joints
and marrow; it judges the thoughts and attitudes of the heart.

Hebrews 4:12

Take the helmet of salvation and the sword
of the Spirit, which is the word of God.

Ephesians 6:17

You have exalted above all things your name and your word.

Psalm 138:2 ESV

Sisterhood

I need to have back surgery after all," Marilyn told me on
the phone.

My friend had been in pain for months. Her doctor had
tried both decompression and cortisone shots, but neither
were making the excruciating pain any easier to bear.

I reassured her that our dear friends and I would be there
for her, not just on the surgery day and the days that followed
but also for as long as it took to get her back on her feet.

On the morning of the surgery, all six of us descended
on the waiting room like a horde of Holsteins. We tend to
be somewhat loud.

"Are you all with Mrs. Meberg?" the nurse asked, clearly
amazed.

"Yes, we are," Luci Swindoll replied.

"Are you *all* family?" she pressed.

"Yes, we are," I said. "We all look a bit different, but we're
sisters!"

Marilyn came through the surgery well, but it took some

time for her to feel strong again. So over the next few weeks, Marilyn's posse took care of every single thing she needed, from rubbing her feet to making her favorite banana pudding to reading to her from one of her favorite books.

What a beautiful example of how God speaks to us through each other. Sometimes, just like with Marilyn and the Holsteins, He speaks to us about how much He loves us and is concerned about our suffering through the compassion and care we offer each other.

He also speaks through His children in other ways. When we are discouraged, we need our brothers and sisters to remind us of the hope we have in Christ. When we are filled with self-condemnation, we need fellow believers to be tangible messages of God's amazing grace. When we wander far from God's great love, we need other believers to gently guide us home.

I am so glad that as a member of the body of Christ, I don't ever have to walk alone, aren't you? I'm going to take some time today to thank God for the gift of my Christian sisters who love me so well. I will also ask Him to fill me with His Spirit so that my heart will be open for Him to speak through me and bring encouragement, grace, and love to my sisters in Christ.

Will you join me?

৵৻ Five Minutes in the Word ৴৶৵

You are the body of Christ, and each one of you is a part of it.

1 Corinthians 12:27

There is one body and one Spirit, just as you were called to one hope
when you were called; one Lord, one faith, one baptism; one God
and Father of all, who is over all and through all and in all.

Ephesians 4:4–6

"My command is this: Love each other as I have loved you."

John 15:12

Above all, love each other deeply, because
love covers over a multitude of sins.

1 Peter 4:8

Be kind and compassionate to one another, forgiving
each other, just as in Christ God forgave you.

Ephesians 4:32

The Song of Creation

What do you think of when you hear the name Saint Francis of Assisi? Perhaps you picture a garden statue holding a small bowl of birdseed. Maybe you remember a story about Saint Francis preaching to the animals.

A friend of mine attends a church that holds special blessings for pets on the day of Saint Francis's feast. Each year, all the church members are invited to bring their pets to the church lawn at 2:00 p.m. to receive their blessing. Except for cats. Cats come at noon!

Saint Francis was more than birdseed and pet blessings. He strongly believed that God reveals Himself to us in His creation. Francis wrote his "Canticle of Creation" on his deathbed. Years of practicing poverty and walking the countryside preaching had left him sick and blind, but in the "Canticle of Creation," Francis saw in his mind's eye God's goodness in all He had made.[14]

The sun, moon, and stars . . .

Fire and water . . .

The earth itself . . .

Have you ever considered that God is speaking to you through His creation? The psalmist certainly believed it was true. Read the first few verses of Psalm 19: "The heavens declare the glory of God; the skies proclaim the work of his hands. Day after day they pour forth speech; night after night they reveal knowledge. They have no speech, they use no words; no sound is heard from them. Yet their voice goes out into all the earth, their words to the ends of the world" (vv. 1–4).

Sometimes, on a particularly beautiful night, I take a blanket outside, lie down, and look up at the stars, flung like diamonds across inky velvet, and this passage fills my heart with praise. I am in awe of the infinite power of our God who placed each and every star in the heavens and calls them all by name. But the beautiful truth about our Father is that this same mighty God thinks about and cares for you and me (Psalm 8:4)!

The God who holds the universe in His hands cares for you and me . . .

I wonder what God wants to say to you today through His creation. Open your window and watch the birds for a while. Slip outside in the darkness of night and gaze at the sky above. Sit by a creek and let the cool water run through your fingers.

And listen.

God is speaking of His majesty and power through all He has made.

> *Through the beauty of His creation, God sings over us.*

～ᘓ Five Minutes in the Word ᘓ～

When I consider your heavens, the work of your fingers, the moon and the stars, which you have set in place, what is mankind that you are mindful of them, human beings that you care for them?
Psalm 8:3–4

Since the creation of the world God's invisible qualities—his eternal power and divine nature—have been clearly seen, being understood from what has been made, so that people are without excuse.
Romans 1:20

*Let the sea resound, and everything in it, the world, and
all who live in it. Let the rivers clap their hands, let the
mountains sing together for joy; let them sing before the LORD.*

Psalm 98:7–9

*The heavens proclaim his righteousness,
and all peoples see his glory.*

Psalm 97:6

*In his hand are the depths of the earth, and the
mountain peaks belong to him. The sea is his, for he
made it, and his hands formed the dry land.*

Psalm 95:4–5

Pass the Bread

When I read a book that speaks deeply to me, I usually order ten more and ask the Holy Spirit to show me when someone I meet might need that message. There can be such companionship in the written word, a sense that you're not alone in your journey.

One such book for me is *The Prisoner in the Third Cell* by Gene Edwards. It's a small book. You can read it in a couple of hours, and I've read it over and over and underlined and dog-eared the pages. I won't give away the story, but it speaks powerfully to times when you wonder where God is and whether He sees your struggle.

Whenever I hear of someone going through a loss that's hard to fathom, I wait for the prompting from God. Then I send a copy of this book with a promise of my prayers.

It is such a mystery to me that the almighty God chooses the writings of mere men and women of faith to speak love into the hearts of His children. It seems like risky business to use such humble tools for a job so important, but that is exactly what He does.

After all, our redeemer God doesn't waste pain. So when one of His children experiences a crushing personal crisis, He walks through it with them and then uses an account of that experience or of the lessons learned to bless others. This sharing is like the breaking of the loaves and fish: authors of life-giving, truth-telling books are passing along to their brothers and sisters a portion of what fed their hungry souls in the wilderness so that others might feast as well.

Through the years many tables of this rich food for the soul have been spread, my friend. Never stop seeking new ones! Ask trusted pastors and Bible teachers which authors they are reading and pick up a new book from time to time. Each evening before bed or early in the morning, reach for one of those books instead of social media or the news. Take a moment to refresh your heart with the truths God has revealed to others on their faith journey.

Those truths may just be the bread you need in the wilderness!

> *Watch for the breadcrumbs the faithful have left along the path.*

❧ Five Minutes in the Word ❧

*Since we are surrounded by such a great cloud of witnesses, let us
throw off everything that hinders and the sin that so easily entangles.
And let us run with perseverance the race marked out for us.*

Hebrews 12:1

*Now we ask you, brothers and sisters, to acknowledge those who work hard
among you, who care for you in the Lord and who admonish you. Hold them in
the highest regard in love because of their work. Live in peace with each other.*

1 Thessalonians 5:12–13

*Even when I am old and gray, do not forsake me, my God, till I declare your
power to the next generation, your mighty acts to all who are to come.*

Psalm 71:18

*God chose the foolish things of the world to shame the wise; God chose the
weak things of the world to shame the strong. God chose the lowly things
of this world and the despised things—and the things that are not—to
nullify the things that are, so that no one may boast before him.*

1 Corinthians 1:27–29

*One generation commends your works to another; they tell of
your mighty acts. They speak of the glorious splendor of your
majesty—and I will meditate on your wonderful works.*

Psalm 145:4–5

Do I Matter?

Vincent van Gogh didn't start out as a master painter. First, he was a minister with the Belgian Evangelical Church. He became a painter because he got fired. You see, van Gogh believed that in order to minister to the desperately poor coal miners to whom he was assigned, he needed to live among them. His superiors disagreed.

One day as van Gogh was conducting a memorial service for fifty-seven men, women, and children who had lost their lives in a mining accident, two representatives from his church arrived at his humble home. When they saw the poverty and squalor, he was fired on the spot for behavior that "undermined the dignity of the priesthood."[5]

So Vincent van Gogh became a painter. Perhaps he understood that God might be served through art as well.

I think Bezalel and Oholiab would have agreed with him. These two men are described in Exodus 31 as skilled artisans who worked on the tent of meeting. God had filled

Bezalel with "the Spirit of God, with wisdom, with understanding, with knowledge and with all kinds of skills—to make artistic designs for work in gold, silver and bronze, to cut and set stones, to work in wood, and to engage in all kinds of crafts" (vv. 3–5). He appointed Oholiab to help him.

I love the fact that Bezalel and Oholiab were not among the priests who served God's house, or the shepherds who raised the livestock for the sacrifices, or the warriors who protected the ornate place of worship filled with silver and gold. Bezalel and Oholiab were artists, and they had an important part to play in God's plan. They mattered.

Have you ever wondered whether *you* matter? What a terrific question to bring before your Creator in the quiet! As you do, take some time to meditate on this passage from Paul's letter to the Romans: "In Christ we, though many, form one body, and each member belongs to all the others. We have different gifts, according to the grace given to each of us" (Romans 12:5–6).

You, like Bezalel and Oholiab, were created by God with unique gifts that will enable you to play an important part in His kingdom!

But that's not all. You also matter because God created

you in love, saved you in love, and adopted you in love. He shaped your body and soul "wonderfully" (Psalm 139:13–14). He sent His Son to give His life for yours and "lavished" you with outrageous love, naming you His very own daughter (1 John 3:1). God gives you worth that nothing can ever diminish.

Get alone with God today and let Him remind you how important you are, both to Him and to all the rest of us in the body of Christ! We need you and your unique gifts for the kingdom of God!

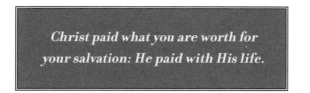

Christ paid what you are worth for your salvation: He paid with His life.

ᕫ Five Minutes in the Word ᕲ

God said, "Let us make mankind in our image, in our likeness, so that they may rule over the fish in the sea and the birds in the sky, over the livestock and all the wild animals, and over all the creatures that move along the ground."

Genesis 1:26

We are God's handiwork, created in Christ Jesus to do good works, which God prepared in advance for us to do.

Ephesians 2:10

"Can a mother forget the baby at her breast and have no compassion on the child she has borne? Though she may forget, I will not forget you! See, I have engraved you on the palms of my hands; your walls are ever before me."

Isaiah 49:15–16

There are different kinds of gifts, but the same Spirit distributes them. There are different kinds of service, but the same Lord. There are different kinds of working, but in all of them and in everyone it is the same God at work.

1 Corinthians 12:4–6

You made all the delicate, inner parts of my body and knit me together in my mother's womb.

Psalm 139:13 NLT

An Inexhaustible
Well of Hope

I met Cindy when she was the producer's assistant on one of my early records (yes, *records* . . . it was awhile ago!). The minute I met her, I knew we'd be friends for life. She made me laugh like few others ever have. I loved her goofy sense of humor. As our friendship deepened over the years, we took trips together, and when we moved to different states, we made a point to stay in each other's lives. We're exactly the same age, so we made great plans for the trip we would take to New York the year we both turned sixty.

So I couldn't believe the words I was hearing the day she called to tell me she was sick. *How could Cindy have lung cancer? She's never smoked in her life!* It felt surreal.

As the cancer spread, we prayed and believed and hoped . . . and watched her get weaker and weaker.

Her memorial service left me breathless. The church

was packed to capacity with people paying tribute to a woman who had served quietly and joyfully behind the scenes.

And the beauty was . . . it wasn't a dark day. It was a celebration. Cindy had run her race and finished well. She was home free!

What a brighter perspective I had that day than when I first heard Cindy's diagnosis.

Sooner or later, most of us will face something that shakes us to our very souls. When that happens, I pray we find ourselves on our knees, holding fast to our Father's goodness and loving embrace, declaring through our tears, "Father, in spite of all of this, You are my hope!"

Cindy's life and death show us that for the child of God, He is always our hope, to the very brink of the grave . . . and beyond. In the Old Testament, Job knew that truth. He lost pretty much everything—his wealth, his health, his precious children—yet at his very lowest point he said the most remarkable thing: "I know that my redeemer lives, and that in the end he will stand on the earth. And after my skin has been destroyed, yet in my flesh I will see God; I myself will see him with my own eyes. . . . How my heart yearns within me!" (Job 19:25–27).

Job knew the inexhaustible well of hope available to the child of God. It extends beyond anything this world can throw your way. It can sustain you, no matter what you encounter. It reaches well beyond the depths of the grave.

Yes, my dear sister, He is our hope!

Take your troubles and your grief straight into your Father's presence. Pour everything out at His feet. Then, when your tears are spent, linger in the quiet for a while and let the Father remind you that your Redeemer lives and your hope is sure.

> *"My hope is built on nothing less than Jesus' blood and righteousness."*

ᗖᑢ Five Minutes in the Word ᑤᗕ

God will never forget the needy; the hope of the afflicted will never perish.

Psalm 9:18

Wait for the LORD; be strong and take heart and wait for the LORD.

Psalm 27:14

A horse is a vain hope for deliverance; despite all its great strength it cannot save. But the eyes of the LORD are on those who fear him, on those whose hope is in his unfailing love, to deliver them from death and keep them alive in famine.

Psalm 33:17–19

I wait for the LORD, my whole being waits, and in his word I put my hope. I wait for the Lord more than watchmen wait for the morning, more than watchmen wait for the morning.

Psalm 130:5–6

Now, LORD, what do I look for? My hope is in you.

Psalm 39:7

A Beautiful Ending

The emperor of China had a problem. Something was destroying his mulberry trees. So he did what any brilliant man does when faced with a problem he can't handle: he turned it over to his wife!

When Empress Ce Ling Shee looked at the trees, she noticed a moth laying eggs on the mulberry leaves, eggs that of course hatched into caterpillars. After a few days, each caterpillar spun a thread that it wrapped itself in, forming a cocoon. The empress plucked one of the cocoons from the leaves and dropped it in hot water. Slowly, the delicate and beautiful thread began to unwind. It was a half mile long when the empress stretched it out and measured it! Then it occurred to her: perhaps this thread could be woven into cloth.

And that was the moment the silk trade was born. An empire of extraordinary beauty and wealth began with an emperor's garden disaster![16]

Sometimes it's difficult to envision a positive outcome when we're in the middle of a mess. We look out onto the garden of our lives, find it in ruins, and feel helpless. We don't even know where to begin to make things right. How could the emperor have ever imagined—and *how could we imagine*—that unfathomable beauty and blessing could rise out of the thing that seemed to be his destruction?

But making beautiful endings out of impossible situations is God's specialty. He never wastes a single trial. He transforms it *all* for our good and His glory. Read these words from 1 Peter 1: "In all this you greatly rejoice, though now for a little while you may have had to suffer grief in all kinds of trials. These have come so that the proven genuineness of your faith—of greater worth than gold . . . may result in praise, glory and honor when Jesus Christ is revealed" (vv. 6–7).

If we keep following the light of God's presence through this dark and difficult world, we will see God turn around our impossible messes! That's His promise! Nothing can stop the amazing redemptive power of our God.

So come.

Bring it all to the Weaver of beautiful endings . . .

The worst heartbreak . . .

The most difficult failures . . .

The most painful days . . .

The Enemy may throw every weapon he has at you, but he is not the one who gets to write the end of your story.

> *It's amazing what God will do with a broken life if you give Him all the pieces.*

⤜ Five Minutes in the Word ⤛

We know that in all things God works for the good of those who love him, who have been called according to his purpose.

Romans 8:28

The Spirit of the Sovereign LORD is on me, because the LORD has anointed me . . . to bestow on them a crown of beauty instead of ashes, the oil of joy instead of mourning, and a garment of praise instead of a spirit of despair.

Isaiah 61:1, 3

Consider it pure joy, my brothers and sisters, whenever you face trials of many kinds, because you know that the testing of your faith produces perseverance. Let perseverance finish its work so that you may be mature and complete, not lacking anything.

James 1:2–4

"I will repay you for the years the locusts have eaten."

Joel 2:25

"Blessed are you when people hate you, when they exclude you and insult you and reject your name as evil, because of the Son of Man. Rejoice in that day and leap for joy, because great is your reward in heaven. For that is how their ancestors treated the prophets."

Luke 6:22–23

A Day Off

Do you ever feel that if you are asked to do one more thing you will physically combust? I've definitely had those moments.

I recently read an article about the exhausted American workforce. It mentioned a young working mother who was stretched so thin that she always entered the cook time on the microwave as 1:11, 2:22, or 3:33, instead of 1:00, 2:00, or 3:00. Hitting the same key repeatedly saved her time.[17]

Yowser! That is one stretched-thin woman!

And she isn't alone. Maybe you're reading this and thinking, *What a great idea! I think I'll start cooking like that!* I hope you don't feel that pressed for time, but even if you don't, you're probably still overworked and deeply tired.

What if I could give you a day off? Not just from work but also from the burdens of your soul, to-do lists, and "should've"s? What if I said that, as a bonus, you had permission to shut out all the voices that are screaming at you to buy more, do more, *be more*?

The only thing for you to do on this day would be to rest in God's presence and hear from Him how much He loves you. You would spend quiet time with Him, worship Him, and get outside. You would spend quality time with your family and friends, maybe share a great meal together and linger at the table. At the end of this beautiful day of recharging, you would find your strength and courage renewed for the week ahead.

Sounds like a dream, doesn't it?

But it isn't a dream. It's called the Sabbath.

As a culture, we've gotten away from observing the Sabbath. Maybe it was because some of us grew up under a legalistic observation of it. I understand. I'm certainly not suggesting legalism. God never meant for the Sabbath to be a burden.

But we miss something when we completely dismiss it. Without this special time set apart to be with God and hear from Him, our hearts grow dry and weary. One Jewish theologian said it beautifully: "Six days a week we wrestle with the world, wringing profits from the earth; on the Sabbath we especially care for the seed of eternity planted in the soul."[8]

Reconsider God's gift of Sabbath. You may feel like you'll be endlessly behind if you take this time away from your responsibilities, but I promise you that a recharging takes place when you observe the Sabbath—a recharging that simply doesn't happen any other way.

God gave you the gift of the Sabbath because He loves you. I think it's time to open that gift!

> *Spirit, help me observe a Sabbath—in a step of faith that things that need to get done will get done.*

～ Five Minutes in the Word ～

His delight is in the law of the LORD, and in His law he meditates day and night. He shall be like a tree planted by the rivers of water, that brings forth its fruit in its season, whose leaf also shall not wither.

Psalm 1:2–3 NKJV

In vain you rise early and stay up late, toiling for food to eat—for he grants sleep to those he loves.

Psalm 127:2

"Observe the Sabbath day by keeping it holy,
as the Lord *your God has commanded you."*

Deuteronomy 5:12

Yes, my soul, find rest in God; my hope comes from him. Truly
he is my rock and my salvation; he is my fortress, I will not
be shaken. My salvation and my honor depend on God; he
is my mighty rock, my refuge. Trust in him at all times, you
people; pour out your hearts to him, for God is our refuge.

Psalm 62:5–8

"Watch out! Be on your guard against all kinds of greed;
life does not consist in the abundance of possessions."

Luke 12:15

What Is My Worth?

I t's not real!" she declared.

Eighteen-year-old Essena O'Neill sobbed as she looked into the camera to record her final YouTube video. She had spent the previous six years devoting her life to her social media presence. Along the way, she had gathered more than five hundred thousand Instagram followers and a modeling contract. Maintaining her image had become her career, and now she was walking away from it all.

"I quit social media for my twelve-year-old self," she said. "When I was twelve, I told myself that I was worth nothing because I wasn't popular online or beautiful by society's standards."[19]

I ache for the number of young girls who judge their worth by our culture's flawed standards. If only that lack of self-worth ended with adolescence! It too often bleeds into our adulthood, and we continue to judge our worth by what we see in the mirror.

It's actually an age-old issue. In the Victorian Age, a woman's worth was strongly connected to how well-mannered she was or whether she found a good husband. In the 1950s, the ideal woman kept house perfectly and had the kids in order and dinner on the table when her husband walked through the front door after work—and she did all this while wearing lipstick, heels, and pearls. That's just wrong, people!

Although women today have many more opportunities to explore their gifts, social media puts ridiculous pressure on girls and women to concentrate on and perfect their image. Even after you take a selfie on your phone, you can download apps to make yourself look better. This focus on appearance is out of control. As an old TV commercial for cameras put it, "Today, image is everything."

What a cruel way to judge ourselves and each other.

Image, you see, is most certainly *not* everything. It is fleeting and empty, and very often—as Essena painfully pointed out—it's just not real.

So where are we to find a legitimate answer to that heart cry, *What am I worth?*

We take our question to the only One who really has a right to weigh in on it in the first place: we go to our Maker!

And to Him, we matter more than we can even grasp. After all, He carefully formed us with His own hands (Psalm 139:13). We are so precious to Him that His eyes have never left us, not even for a moment (Psalm 34:15). And to Him, we are a treasure of such great worth that He gave His only Son to remove the sins that kept us distanced from Him (John 3:16).

Don't wound your soul by allowing the wrong people to determine your worth. Instead, listen to your Father's voice and to His alone.

Today I declare that I am a beloved daughter of God.

⤷ Five Minutes in the Word ↩

"Indeed, the very hairs of your head are all numbered.
Don't be afraid; you are worth more than many sparrows."

Luke 12:7

You created my inmost being; you knit me together in my mother's womb.

Psalm 139:13

My frame was not hidden from you when I was made in the secret

place, when I was woven together in the depths of the earth.

Psalm 139:15

No one can redeem the life of another or give to God a ransom for

them—the ransom for a life is costly, no payment is ever enough.

Psalm 49:7–8

We wait for the blessed hope—the appearing of the glory of our

great God and Savior, Jesus Christ, who gave himself for us

to redeem us from all wickedness and to purify for himself a

people that are his very own, eager to do what is good.

Titus 2:13–14

Holy Habits

Tink is my funny little Bichon, and she is a creature of habit. Every morning after she has breakfast, she trots her little self over to the cabinet where we keep dog treats. I have about two minutes to retrieve a snack before she becomes extremely verbal. Sometimes I move slowly just to get Tink's whole performance.

She'll approach me and stare. If that doesn't work, there will be one short yet pointed bark. If that fails, she will back up and reapproach me with an intensity utterly disproportional to her size. I think we could take this show on the road!

This morning routine is a curious habit Tink has gotten into, and so are some of my own habits.

Habits are powerful. Pulitzer Prize–winning poet Mary Oliver wrote, "The patterns of our lives reveal us. Our habits measure us."[20] Ms. Oliver is right. When we take time to think about our habits honestly, we are able to see pretty quickly what we love most.

But I believe our good habits also have the power to *shape* our loves. They can be tools to strengthen us in our walk with God.

Take a moment to imagine how your relationship with God would be enriched if you consciously developed some holy habits that put you in His presence, even for just a moment, several times throughout the day.

Now, before you get overwhelmed, I am not talking about a huge amount of time here. What I do regularly throughout the day is just stop what I'm doing, turn my heart toward my heavenly Father, and thank Him for His love.

I would love to be able to say this is my original idea, but it isn't. It is as old as church history. It's the same heart behind commonplace practices such as morning and evening prayers and Bible reading.

Morning and evening are still a great place to begin. At nighttime I love to write a gratitude list. (Saying "thank you" can shift our perspective!) Mealtimes are good cues to turn our hearts to God too. What is most important, though, is that your holy habits work for you. Try a few different practices until something feels right.

When we develop holy habits that get us into God's presence, He will meet us there, and we will find sweet refreshment for our souls!

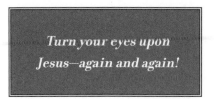

*Turn your eyes upon
Jesus—again and again!*

⇌ Five Minutes in the Word ⇌

*My voice You shall hear in the morning, O Lord. In the
morning I will direct it to You. And I will look up.*

Psalm 5:3 NKJV

I will sing of your strength, in the morning I will sing of your love.

Psalm 59:16

I cry to you for help, Lord; in the morning my prayer comes before you.

Psalm 88:13

*Satisfy us in the morning with your unfailing love, that
we may sing for joy and be glad all our days.*

Psalm 90:14

*May my prayer be set before you like incense; may the
lifting up of my hands be like the evening sacrifice.*

Psalm 141:2

The Seasons Belong to Him

Have you noticed that Christmas has begun to feel a little bit like a battleground?

Which camp are you in—Happy Holidays or Merry Christmas? What design is on the Starbucks cup this year? Did someone just inject Frosty the Snowman into my favorite carol?

I'm not trying to fuel the controversy, but I would like to suggest that maybe—just maybe—the struggle is a symptom of a deeper longing. And I think it's a longing to return to the true meaning of our Christian holidays.

If you're like me, you don't want to fight about Christmas. You don't need it to be "us versus them" on any issue. You just want your celebration to be meaningful. You want it to be about Jesus.

Traditional Christian holidays are special opportunities to be intentional about entering God's presence for a season—whether it is Christmas, Easter, or Lent. In fact, isn't the original purpose of these holidays to set aside a special time to remember what God has done for us and give Him thanks?

These times offer special opportunities to refresh our hearts in God's presence, but how can we recapture that simplicity during Christian holidays that have been virtually overrun by commercialism?

I have a couple of ideas. First, we can commit to simplifying our lives during these times. We need to say no to some activities that drain us so we can say yes to others that feed our souls.

I also like to draw nearer to God during these meaningful holidays by attending special services at my church.

And I have a collection of books with daily readings for each season. (If you aren't sure what to read, ask around. Many churches or Christian authors offer seasonal reading lists for just this purpose.)

Whatever you choose, even if it's just a moment of quiet reflection as you wait in the carpool lane, I pray you'll find the season reclaimed and your heart renewed. After all, the seasons—and all our days—belong to Him!

> *In the midst of the noise,*
> *I will find You in the quiet.*

❧ Five Minutes in the Word ❧

God said, *"Let there be lights in the vault of the sky to separate the day from the night, and let them serve as signs to mark sacred times, and days and years."*

Genesis 1:14

He made the moon to mark the seasons, and the sun knows when to go down. You bring darkness, it becomes night, and all the beasts of the forest prowl.

Psalm 104:19–20

He changes times and seasons; he deposes kings and raises up others. He gives wisdom to the wise and knowledge to the discerning.

Daniel 2:21

He has not left himself without testimony: He has shown kindness by giving you rain from heaven and crops in their seasons; he provides you with plenty of food and fills your hearts with joy.

Acts 14:17

Worship the LORD in the splendor of his holiness; tremble before him, all the earth.

Psalm 96:9

Healing for the Deepest Wounds

She just needed a little money to finish college.

The price was steep, but she reasoned to herself that she wouldn't pay it for long. She was only ten units away from earning her degree.

But the price is always steeper than expected when the Enemy is offering the solution to our problems. Before she knew it, she was the one wearing a price tag.

When she finally escaped the man who had trafficked her, she still didn't have the money for college. Instead, she was completely broken and had a baby on the way. It was difficult to believe that anyone or anything had the power to heal her heart's deepest wounds.

Then Jesus stepped in.

"He helped me to see that I could never be too far gone and that He came to die for people just like me," she said.

"When I thought He had given up on me, I look back now and realize that in my darkest moments, He was right there next to me."[21]

I don't know what wounds you carry, but maybe you have doubts about whether they can be healed, like this young woman did. *Am I too far gone? Has God given up on me?*

Maybe your heartbreak is so overwhelming that you can't imagine healing and relief. I understand. I've been there. But this truth is eternal: *nothing is too hard for God.*

God wanted to be sure you knew this was true, so He included in Scripture countless stories of shattered lives that He made whole.

David had a child through adultery and had his lover's husband murdered, yet he went on to become known as a man after God's own heart. Mary Magdalene was possessed by demons, yet she was delivered from them and, later, was the first to see the risen Christ! The Samaritan woman had a long line of broken relationships, and her bad reputation made her a social outcast. But after she met Christ, she became the first missionary to her village.

We could go on and on to make this point: God restores people.

What about you? Do you want to know that God's healing power is enough for you too? Come into His presence and risk asking this question: "My God, can You heal the deepest wounds of my heart?"

Then open your heart to hear His sweet response: "All things are possible with [Me]" (Mark 10:27).

> *There is no place so dark that the love of Christ can't find you and heal you.*

⸙ Five Minutes in the Word ⸙

Restore to me the joy of your salvation and grant me a willing spirit, to sustain me.

Psalm 51:12

Though you have made me see troubles, many and bitter, you will restore my life again; from the depths of the earth you will again bring me up.

Psalm 71:20

Have mercy on me, LORD, for I am faint;
heal me, LORD, for my bones are in agony.
Psalm 6:2

Heal me, LORD, and I will be healed; save me
and I will be saved, for you are the one I praise.
Jeremiah 17:14

"The word of God will never fail."
Luke 1:37 NLT

He lifted me out of the pit of despair, out of
the mud and the mire. He set my feet on solid
ground and steadied me as I walked along.
Psalm 40:2 NLT

Trust Fall

This is an exercise in team building," our camp leader told us. "Over the next week you're going to have to be able to trust each other as we learn survival skills in the wild."

I wasn't sure why we had to learn how to survive in the wild when we had perfectly good cabins at the campground!

"I'd like you to pair up as we practice the trust fall," she said.

I wasn't very keen on those two words . . . *trust* and *fall*. I much preferred *campfires* and *s'mores*, but she seemed determined.

We lined up with our partners' backs facing us, and after she counted to three, they fell back into our arms.

"Now switch," she said.

I stretched out my arms like a prima ballerina, but as I fell my partner violently sneezed, and I landed flat on my rear end in the mud. Trust me to have the only partner with allergies!

The truth is, in real life, even people we trust will sometimes let us down.

Jesus isn't like that. He is perfectly trustworthy! I am so glad, because there are times when I find myself wishing He would give me more details about *the plan*. It would be so helpful if He would lay out a nice presentation about how everything is going to unfold. Then I could make a few suggestions and sign off on the whole thing.

But that isn't how God usually operates. Instead, He seems to prefer to give us wisdom and grace for each moment as it comes. We see that vividly in the story of Joseph as he journeys from a beloved son to a lowly slave, from being wrongfully imprisoned to being elevated to the second-highest official in Egypt. Joseph had no idea where his story would lead him, but he remained faithful and trusted God to protect him and comfort him.

And in the end, when his brothers were bowing down before him, just as Joseph's dream had prophesied so many years before, he was able to say with confidence in the goodness of his Lord: "You intended to harm me, but God intended it for good to accomplish what is now being done" (Genesis 50:20).

Oh, that we would be able to place that kind of trust in our Father, knowing that He is always working everything together for our good and that His plans are always better than any we could create on our own.

Let's stop everything else for just a moment to marvel at God's goodness.

Let's remember how He's shown Himself trustworthy in our lives.

Let's ask Him for the guidance, wisdom, and grace only He can give, and praise Him because He is good.

And let's fall into His arms, knowing that He will always be there to catch us!

> *We can always trust in our good and wise Father who loves us with an everlasting love.*

ᷓ Five Minutes in the Word ᷓ

"My thoughts are not your thoughts, neither are your ways my ways," declares the LORD.

Isaiah 55:8

*Jesus replied, "You do not realize now what
I am doing, but later you will understand."*
John 13:7

*Trust in the LORD with all your heart and
lean not on your own understanding.*
Proverbs 3:5

*Faith is confidence in what we hope for
and assurance about what we do not see.*
Hebrews 11:1

*Jesus told him, "Because you have seen me, you have believed;
blessed are those who have not seen and yet have believed."*
John 20:29

Let All the Earth Be Silent

L inda! Linda, just *listen* to me!"

Three-year-old Mateo was clearly getting frustrated with his mom. Apparently he thought he would be more persuasive if he used her first name!

When she said, "No cupcakes," Mateo disagreed. After all, he was at *Grandma's* house, and everybody knows Grandma makes the rules at her house, not Mom.

Mateo's mom wanted to set her little boy straight, but each time she began to correct him, Mateo protested with "Linda! Linda! Listen to me!"[22]

Obviously Mateo's mom found some humor in the whole thing because she recorded it and posted it on YouTube. From there it went viral and eventually found its way to me.

I thought Mateo was a riot, but after a few moments I quit laughing because I began to wonder if I ever act a bit like Mateo in my prayers. Am I too often so concerned with being heard that I miss what God is saying? Is He speaking, but I can't hear Him because I never embrace the silence?

I don't think I'm the only one. Sometimes it seems our world is afraid of silence. It seems like almost every moment of the day is filled with motion and sound. Even in the middle of the night, our phones buzz and beep.

The Bible encourages us to practice periods of silence before God. I love this verse from Habakkuk: "The LORD is in his holy temple; let all the earth be silent before him" (Habakkuk 2:20).

Wow . . . isn't that beautiful?

Does silence still matter in a world addicted to noise? I think it matters more than ever because practicing silence before God clears the way for Him to speak to us.

If you are new to this practice, you might find it challenging at first, but be patient with yourself. Begin by finding a quiet place where you won't be interrupted. Then give yourself permission to put everything aside for just a few minutes—your worries, to-do lists, whatever you need to do next—and be silent before God.

You might find it easier to keep your mind on God if you repeat to yourself a simple truth such as "God loves me" or "I belong to Jesus." Or you can also try repeating a simple prayer like "Christ, have mercy" or "Jesus, fill me with Your love."

If your mind wanders, don't beat yourself up. Just gently bring your heart and mind back to Jesus.

He's waiting there for you always . . . with love . . . with mercy . . . with forgiveness and grace.

Let all the earth be silent before Him.

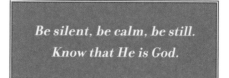

Be silent, be calm, be still.
Know that He is God.

ꙮ Five Minutes in the Word ꙮ

Be silent before the Sovereign LORD, for the day of the LORD is near. The
LORD has prepared a sacrifice; he has consecrated those he has invited.
Zephaniah 1:7

Set a guard over my mouth, LORD; keep watch over the door of my lips.
Psalm 141:3

*Those who consider themselves religious and yet
do not keep a tight rein on their tongues deceive
themselves, and their religion is worthless.*

James 1:26

*Sin is not ended by multiplying words,
but the prudent hold their tongues.*

Proverbs 10:19

*Tremble and do not sin; when you are on
your beds, search your hearts and be silent.*

Psalm 4:4

Choosing Gratitude

When Joshua Kaufman survived Hitler's brutal concentration camp in Dachau, he had only one wish: he wanted to thank one of the United States soldiers who had liberated him. Joshua waited seventy years for that moment . . .

Eighty-nine-year-old Daniel Gillespie was making his way across the street. The soldier who had entered Dachau as a strong, young man to set Joshua free now moved slowly, carefully navigating his walker over the pavement. When the two men drew close, Joshua saluted Daniel, took his hand and kissed it, and then kissed him on the cheek.

Joshua's voice was choked with emotion as he addressed the man who had freed him so long ago. "Then I didn't have the strength to kiss your feet," he said to Daniel. "I was too weak. I will do it now." Joshua carefully moved Daniel's walker to the side so that he could drop to his knees and kiss the tops of Daniel's shoes.[23]

Gratitude is a tremendous force. In fact, our gratitude to God invites Him into our lives to frame even our deepest wounds in the grace of Christ.

Yet gratitude doesn't come naturally, especially during difficult times. Grumbling, complaining, and focusing on all that's wrong is far easier than choosing to focus on the good in our lives and to be thankful. That's why we need to approach gratitude as a discipline: we choose gratitude because God tells us to.

Over and over in the Psalms, David encouraged himself to praise God no matter how hard life was. He did this because even when life was difficult and painful, God was good.

Approaching God with gratitude—recalling His generous kindnesses to us, past and present—helps us remember that truth. Giving Him thanks opens our hearts to His love and His voice and leads us to rest in His presence. It's a wonderful way to begin our quiet time with God.

So let's practice gratitude right now. We can start with everyday items—the food we eat, the clothes we wear, even the ability to take another breath—and go from there. As we count our blessings, we will find that the good in our lives shines brighter than ever before and that our hearts begin to open more widely to receive all that God longs to speak into us.

The Enemy of our souls would keep us in a concentration camp of bitterness about what we do not have, but the cross of Christ proclaims that He has won the victory and that we are free to "enter his gates with thanksgiving and his courts with praise" (Psalm 100:4).

> *Gratitude opens doors that lead us out of bitterness and into joy.*

⁓⟨ Five Minutes in the Word ⟩⁓

Godliness with contentment is great gain. For we brought nothing into the world, and we can take nothing out of it. But if we have food and clothing, we will be content with that.
1 Timothy 6:6–8

I have learned in whatever situation I am to be content. I know how to be brought low, and I know how to abound. In any and every circumstance, I have learned the secret of facing plenty and hunger, abundance and need. I can do all things through him who strengthens me.
Philippians 4:11–13 ESV

Shout with joy to the LORD, all the earth! Worship the LORD with gladness. Come before him, singing with joy. Acknowledge that the LORD is God! He made us, and we are his. We are his people, the sheep of his pasture. Enter his gates with thanksgiving; go into his courts with praise. Give thanks to him and praise his name. For the LORD is good. His unfailing love continues forever, and his faithfulness continues to each generation.

Psalm 100 NLT

Let the message of Christ dwell among you richly as you teach and admonish one another with all wisdom through psalms, hymns, and songs from the Spirit, singing to God with gratitude in your hearts.

Colossians 3:16

I will praise God's name in song and glorify him with thanksgiving.

Psalm 69:30

The Expectation
of His Presence

If you follow me on Facebook, you are, perhaps, painfully aware of one fact about me: I love to post pictures and videos of our three little dogs.

My favorite time to film them is when Barry and I pick them up at the kennel after we've been on a trip. I sit on the floor facing the door where those furry wigglers will emerge. When I hear their familiar barks, I press Record, and the moment they see me on the floor, they throw themselves at me. My videos are usually short because they tend to knock my phone out of my hand. Their unrestrained joy makes my heart glad!

And their unrestrained joy is the kind of joy I want to have when I enter into God's presence. Now, I don't want to knock Him over, but I do want my heart to overflow with unfiltered joy whenever I enter His presence! I want my heart to ache with the expectation of His nearness.

That expectation is grounded in this glorious truth: Jesus promised us God will be faithful to give us the good gift of His presence. In Luke 11, Jesus told a parable about a father and his son: "Which of you fathers, if your son asks for a fish, will give him a snake instead? . . . If you then, though you are evil, know how to give good gifts to your children, how much more will your Father in heaven give the Holy Spirit to those who ask him!" (vv. 11, 13).

In this passage Jesus was teaching that the greatest gift we can ever receive is the gift of the Holy Spirit, the Comforter, the Counselor, the Guide, the One God sent to reveal Himself to us. Jesus told His disciples that it was actually good for them that He was going back to the Father because when He did, the Holy Spirit would come (John 16:7). No longer would God walk beside them in human flesh; He would actually dwell within them—and, centuries later, within us.

That is the promise, and God keeps His promises! So come into His presence with confidence and joy and expect Him to meet you there!

> *Run into the arms of your Father with
> unbridled joy and be swept up in His love.*

⮿ Five Minutes in the Word ⮾

*I say to myself, "The LORD is my portion; therefore I will wait for
him." The LORD is good to those whose hope is in him, to the one who
seeks him; it is good to wait quietly for the salvation of the LORD.*
Lamentations 3:24–26

*I am still confident of this: I will see the
goodness of the LORD in the land of the living.*
Psalm 27:13

*This is the confidence we have in approaching God: that if we ask
anything according to his will, he hears us. And if we know that he hears
us—whatever we ask—we know that we have what we asked of him.*
1 John 5:14–15

*We have come to share in Christ, if indeed we hold
our original conviction firmly to the very end.*
Hebrews 3:14

A Whisper in the Wilderness

Have you ever needed to hear a word from God more than you needed *anything*?

Elijah was in just that place. He was physically, spiritually, and emotionally exhausted. Even worse, Queen Jezebel, the supervillain of her day, had sent him word that she was going to kill him in the next twenty-four hours.

Poor Elijah was so discouraged that he couldn't see the light at the end of the tunnel anymore. As a matter of fact, when I read 1 Kings 19, I see a man who is so at the end of himself that he doesn't even *know* what he needs to feel better. I totally get that!

But God knew. What Elijah needed most was to hear from Him. When we read about what happens next, we learn a valuable lesson about how to recognize the voice of God.

God told Elijah to get ready because He was about to pass by. First, there was a violent wind—so powerful it broke apart the mountain and shattered rocks. But God wasn't in the wind. Next, there was an earthquake, but God wasn't in the earthquake either. After the earthquake, there was a fire, and God wasn't in the fire. Then, after all of these loud, powerful events, there came a gentle whisper.

And that was the voice of God.

You might wonder how you will recognize the voice of God when He speaks to you. Most often, He speaks gently, as He did to Elijah. It will be a soft nudging in your heart.

There are two other important things to remember about the voice of God. First, He will never speak anything to you that contradicts the truth of Scripture. And His voice always speaks loving words. He never condemns—though He may convict our hearts of our sins so that we turn back to Him. His words will offer grace and hope, while the Enemy's words bring condemnation and fear. God speaks words of life!

I hope you are as encouraged by Elijah's story as I am. I'm thankful that God speaks in all kinds of situations, including when I am worn-out and too discouraged even to know what I need. I am especially thankful that although God is all-powerful, He speaks to me gently.

Oh, what a kind and gracious God!

> *The Lord is close to the*
> *brokenhearted and rescues them.*

~⟨~ Five Minutes in the Word ~⟩~

After the fire came a gentle whisper. When Elijah heard it, he pulled
his cloak over his face and went out and stood at the mouth of the
cave. Then a voice said to him, "What are you doing here, Elijah?"

1 Kings 19:12–13

She gave this name to the LORD who spoke to her: "You are the God
who sees me," for she said, "I have now seen the One who sees me."

Genesis 16:13

God spoke to Israel in a vision at night and said, . . . "I am God,
the God of your father," he said, "Do not be afraid to go down
to Egypt, for I will make you into a great nation there."

Genesis 46:2–3

The words of the LORD are flawless, like silver
purified in a crucible, like gold refined seven times.

Psalm 12:6

By the word of the LORD the heavens were made, their starry host by the breath of his mouth. . . . Let all the earth fear the LORD; let all the people of the world revere him. For he spoke, and it came to be; he commanded, and it stood firm. . . . We wait in hope for the LORD; he is our help and our shield. In him our hearts rejoice, for we trust in his holy name. May your unfailing love be with us, LORD, even as we put our hope in you.

Psalm 33:6, 8–9, 20–22

The LORD is near to all who call on him, to all who call on him in truth. He fulfills the desires of those who fear him; he hears their cry and saves them.

Psalm 145:18–19

Taking a Walk with God

When Christian was a little boy, I could read him like a book. If he'd had a great day at school, he'd be higher than a kite, and if he'd had a bad day, everything about his body language spoke of doom and gloom. The best way to get him to open up was to go for a walk together. As we walked side by side in the fresh air, he would slowly unburden himself.

There is something about taking a walk with God that helps me unburden too, especially when I pay attention to the wonders of His creation.

Whenever I think about the way God speaks to us through creation, I am reminded of Job. Most of us remember that Job went through some devastating trials, but do you remember how God put Job's heart at rest? For four breathtaking chapters, God walked Job through the wonders of His creation, from the vast storehouses of snow to every creature that has ever roamed the earth. He reminded Job that only He, the Creator and Sustainer of life, performs mighty acts like making lightning strike, giving the horse its strength, and commanding the dawn to rise.

After God showed off the wonders of what He had made and the power He had over them, Job found his faith strengthened and renewed: "I know that you can do all things. . . . My ears had heard of you but now my eyes have seen you" (Job 42:2, 5).

That encounter changed everything for Job.

It's one thing to know things *about* God. It's quite another to *know* Him. In the midst of his pain, Job was reminded of the greatness and majesty of God—right there in the world around him. He never would have signed up for such loss and suffering, but that fresh, profound understanding of the heart of His Father brought peace.

Perhaps today you can find a few moments to get away from all that's pressing in on you so you can be reminded that the same God who puts the sun to bed and holds the stars in place is holding you too.

Take a walk with God!

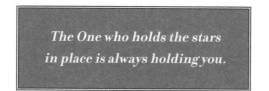

The One who holds the stars in place is always holding you.

✂ Five Minutes in the Word ✂

*LORD, our Lord, how majestic is your name in all the
earth! You have set your glory in the heavens.*

Psalm 8:1

*You built your palace on the ocean deeps, made a chariot out of clouds
and took off on wind-wings. You commandeered winds as messengers,
appointed fire and flame as ambassadors. . . . You blanketed earth with
ocean, covered the mountains with deep waters; then you roared and
the water ran away—your thunder crash put it to flight. Mountains
pushed up, valleys spread out in the places you assigned them. . . .
What a wildly wonderful world, GOD! You made it all, with Wisdom
at your side, made earth overflow with your wonderful creations.*

Psalm 104:3–4, 6–8, 24 THE MESSAGE

*The earth is the LORD's, and everything in it, the world, and all who live in
it; for he founded it upon the seas and established it upon the waters. . . .
Who is he, this King of glory? The LORD Almighty—he is the King of glory.*

Psalm 24:1–2, 10

*The voice of the LORD is over the waters; the God of glory thunders. . . .
The voice of the LORD strikes with flashes of lightning. The voice of*

the LORD shakes the desert; the LORD shakes the Desert of Kadesh. The voice of the LORD twists the oaks and strips the forests bare. And in his temple all cry, "Glory!"

Psalm 29:3, 7–9

I love you, LORD, my strength. . . . As for God, his way is perfect. . . . For who is God besides the LORD? And who is the Rock except our God? It is God who arms me with strength and keeps my way secure. . . . You make your saving help my shield, and your right hand sustains me.

Psalm 18:1, 30–32, 35

I will give thanks to the LORD with all my heart; I will tell of all Your wonders. I will be glad and exult in You; I will sing praise to Your name, O Most High.

Psalm 9:1–2 NASB

Caleb's Gift

How many times had Caleb bounced into the kitchen that morning? His mom had lost count.

My friend's son, Caleb, had just turned eight, and it was the day of his birthday party. The excitement was more than his little heart could handle.

"Hey, buddy," his mom, Samantha, said. "It's going to be a couple hours before your friends get here. I think you need some downtime. Why don't you go find a little quiet?"

Hearing that suggestion, Caleb bounced right out the front door.

A few minutes later, Samantha looked out the kitchen window to see Caleb sitting in the grass with his legs crossed and his eyes closed. She smiled to herself. He certainly seemed to be taking the challenge to "find some quiet" literally!

But as the minutes stretched out and Caleb sat unmoving, Samantha began to wonder if something deeper was going on inside her little boy's heart.

Even at eight, Caleb had a profound understanding of God's love, and he was in fact sitting on the grass listening to his heavenly Father.

Awhile later, when Caleb came back inside the house, he was overwhelmed with emotion.

"Mom, God loves me so much," Caleb said, "and I am so thankful!"

Caleb had received a very special birthday gift. God had spoken to Caleb—given him a sense of His powerful love—as this little one sat quietly in His presence!

How sweet that God speaks to us in so many ways. He speaks through the physical blessings—the food we eat, the clothes we wear, the beauty of creation. He also speaks powerfully through our spiritual blessings—reminding us that He has created us for His glory, redeemed us at great cost, and destined us to live holy lives. What greater gift could a child of God receive than a fresh revelation of these realities?

Our God wants to reach us with His mighty love, which goes deeper and higher than we can imagine. Are we ready to receive it today?

Read Paul's prayer for fellow believers: "[I pray that] you'll be able to take in with all followers of Jesus the extravagant dimensions of Christ's love. Reach out and experience the breadth! Test its length! Plumb the depths! Rise to the heights! Live full lives, full in the fullness of God" (Ephesians 3:14–19 THE MESSAGE).

Take a cue from Caleb today. Stop bouncing off the walls for a little while. Go outside, close your eyes, sit still, and . . . listen.

God wants to tell you that He loves you.

> *In the quiet we will hear God's voice*
> *repeat this wonderful truth: "I love you!"*

﹂ Five Minutes in the Word ﹁

This is how God showed his love among us: He sent his one and
only Son into the world that we might live through him.

1 John 4:9

I have seen you in the sanctuary and beheld your power and your glory.

Psalm 63:2

I will praise you, Lord, among the nations; I will sing of you among
the peoples. For great is your love, reaching to the heavens; your

faithfulness reaches to the skies. Be exalted, O God,
above the heavens; let your glory be over all the earth.
Psalm 57:9–11

Praise be to the God and Father of our Lord Jesus
Christ, who has blessed us in the heavenly realms
with every spiritual blessing in Christ.
Ephesians 1:3

Surely you have granted him unending blessings and
made him glad with the joy of your presence.
Psalm 21:6

"The LORD bless you and keep you; the LORD make his
face shine on you and be gracious to you; and the LORD
turn his face toward you and give you peace."
Numbers 6:24–26

Speaking Sweetly
in the Sorrow

She has been one of my dearest friends for over twenty-five years.

Marlene was one of my bridesmaids. When her dress arrived two sizes too small, she wrapped herself in plastic wrap and cut calories for five days! That's a true friend!

She really is one of a kind. She used to be a hippie and lived in a nudist colony before she came to Christ. (There is nothing about being raised a Scottish Baptist that prepares you for that kind of information—nothing!)

Marlene's deep love for Christ has always challenged and encouraged me, but never more so than when she lost her beloved husband, Frank. I stood beside her as she wrestled with her faith, wept with her as she cried out to God, and have continued to walk with her as she shines even brighter against the background of her dark grief.

God's presence with us through sorrow is both

beautiful and mysterious to me. Sorrow has a way of brushing away the "fluff" from our communication with God. All the externals that seem so important on an average day are wiped away to expose the deepest, truest recesses of our hearts. There is no pretending to have it together in sorrow. No polite prayers. Few distractions. We are direct and focused because *we need God.*

All the pain prepares our hearts to fully hear from Him.

The very fact that God speaks to us in our sorrow is beautiful. When I think of how my powerful God, who created everything I see, is also so tender and gentle that His heart bends toward us when we are hurting . . . I am overwhelmed. We do not serve a callous or faraway God. We belong to a God who cares for the suffering and whose ear is attentive to their cry (Psalm 34:15).

God speaks the most sweetly during our times of sorrow. If that's where you are today, don't hesitate to enter the throne room of your Father in heaven. He is waiting to draw you near and speak words of comfort and healing to your soul.

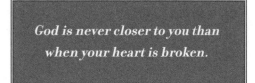

God is never closer to you than when your heart is broken.

❧ Five Minutes in the Word ☙

The eyes of the Lord are on the righteous,
and his ears are attentive to their cry.

Psalm 34:15

Answer me when I call to you, my righteous God. Give me relief
from my distress; have mercy on me and hear my prayer.

Psalm 4:1

Hear my cry, O God; listen to my prayer. From the
ends of the earth I call to you. I call as my heart grows
faint; lead me to the rock that is higher than I.

Psalm 61:1–2

My soul is in deep anguish. How long, Lord, how long? Turn,
Lord, and deliver me; save me because of your unfailing love.

Psalm 6:3–4

We also glory in our sufferings, because we know that suffering produces
perseverance; perseverance, character; and character, hope. And
hope does not put us to shame, because God's love has been poured
out into our hearts by the Holy Spirit, who has been given to us.

Romans 5:3–5

Mission: Possible

Acts 8 reads a little bit like a *Mission: Impossible* type of story . . .

Philip was going about his day when he suddenly received orders from God. Philip's mission, should he choose to accept it, was to leave home and rendezvous at a prearranged destination with a member of the Ethiopian royal court. Once he spotted his target, Philip was to intercept him and share a message that would radically transform the man's life.

It really would have been an impossible mission if Philip were in it all alone, but he wasn't. He had the Holy Spirit on his side.

Actually, the Holy Spirit was *critical* in this mission: His word set it in motion, He prepared the heart of the Ethiopian traveler, He gave Philip step-by-step instructions, and He supplied Philip with the life-changing words of truth.

Philip's *Mission: Impossible* story is a perfect example of how God speaks through His Holy Spirit, but the Holy Spirit has played an important part in human history from the beginning. In Genesis 1:1–2, we see Him at the very dawn of time. When the world was still dark, "formless and empty," the Holy Spirit was there, "hovering over the waters."

Over and over, the book of Judges speaks of the Spirit of the Lord empowering the judges to deliver Israel from her oppressors, and Jesus said that the Holy Spirit spoke through King David in the psalms (Matthew 22:43).

Then something amazing happened on the day of pentecost. Before that day, when the disciples had realized that Jesus would be returning to His Father, they had been heartbroken. After three years of living daily life with the Son of God, they must have wondered how they would make it without Him. But Jesus had said the most astonishing thing: once He returned to His Father, the Holy Spirit would come, and that would be even better than Him being with them! The Holy Spirit would teach them and remind them of all Jesus had taught them (John 14:26).

The day of pentecost was the day Jesus' promise came true. "A sound like the blowing of a violent wind came from heaven and filled the whole house where [the disciples] were sitting. . . . All of them were filled with the Holy Spirit" (Acts 2:2, 4). And they went on to do mighty things in Him!

The Holy Spirit has been speaking to Jesus' people ever since—teaching, leading, and empowering Christians to live vibrant lives for the glory of God.

We've seen the Spirit work in Philip's life. What about yours? And mine?

When the Holy Spirit has a specific mission for us, I pray He'll find us listening for His voice. May we, like Philip, be ready when the Spirit calls and be eager to obey.

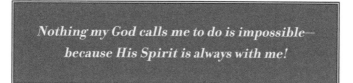

Nothing my God calls me to do is impossible— because His Spirit is always with me!

⟶ Five Minutes in the Word ⟵

"In the last days, God says, I will pour out my Spirit on all people. Your sons and daughters will prophesy, your young men will see visions, your old men will dream dreams. Even on my servants, both men and women, I will pour out my Spirit in those days, and they will prophesy."

Acts 2:17–18

Don't you know that you yourselves are God's temple
and that God's Spirit dwells in your midst?
1 Corinthians 3:16

You yourselves are our letter, written on our hearts, known and read
by everyone. You show that you are a letter from Christ, the result
of our ministry, written not with ink but with the Spirit of the living
God, not on tablets of stone but on tablets of human hearts.
2 Corinthians 3:2–3

I pray that out of his glorious riches he may strengthen
you with power through his Spirit in your inner being, so
that Christ may dwell in your hearts through faith.
Ephesians 3:16–17

"Whenever you are arrested and brought to trial, do not worry
beforehand about what to say. Just say whatever is given you
at the time, for it is not you speaking, but the Holy Spirit."
Mark 13:11

[Ask] God, the glorious Father of our Lord Jesus
Christ, to give you spiritual wisdom and insight so
that you may grow in your knowledge of God.
Ephesians 1:17 NLT

Through the Gates of Praise

One of the first things our son, Christian, did when he started college was to find a church he could call home. That made this mom's heart very happy. A couple of weeks before Christmas, he asked Barry and me to join him for the Sunday service that featured the children's nativity play. It was priceless! Joseph fell off the stage and two shepherds kept dropping their sheep, but it was all those little voices raised together in praise that brought tears to my eyes. There is something precious about children who love their Lord.

That's why I love the story about a group of children erupting in spontaneous praise of Jesus. Matthew 21:15 says, "The children [were] shouting in the temple courts, 'Hosanna to the Son of David.'"

The Scriptures go on to explain that the chief priests and teachers of the law weren't at all happy when they heard those words. They took their complaint to Jesus Himself with, it seems, the expectation that He should put a stop to it. Jesus' response was beautiful: "Have you never read, 'From the lips of children and infants you, Lord, have called forth your praise'?" (v. 16).

These children knew something important: one way we enter into the presence of God is through the gates of praise.

Praise clears away the clutter from our daily lives and prepares our hearts to meet God. It reminds us of all the ways He has met our needs in the past, and it strengthens our faith for the days ahead. When we praise God, we take our rightful place in the great chorus of creation—a chorus that praises Him without ceasing, right alongside the cherubim and seraphim in the very courts of heaven.

There will be times when praising God is the last thing you feel like doing, but give it a try anyway. Start with a whisper if that's all you can manage. Read a psalm aloud if you can't find any words of your own.

However small the offering seems—and even if it's mixed with tears—enter His courts with praise.

> *Praise is a pathway into the presence of God.*

⁓ Five Minutes in the Word ⁓

Worship the LORD with gladness; come before him with joyful songs.

Psalm 100:2

Ascribe to the LORD the glory due his name; worship
the LORD in the splendor of his holiness.

Psalm 29:2

Come, let us bow down in worship, let us kneel before the LORD our Maker; for
he is our God and we are the people of his pasture, the flock under his care.

Psalm 95:6–7

Great is the LORD and most worthy of praise; he is to be feared above all gods.

Psalm 96:4

Ascribe to the LORD the glory due his name; bring
an offering and come into his courts.

Psalm 96:8

The Hindrance
of Abundance

Have you ever thought that winning the lottery would be a fast track to happiness? Many people do. In fact, winning the lottery seemed like a gift from above for the sixteen employees of a power plant in Pennsylvania. But for one of them—William "Bud" Post—the sudden abundance brought devastating unhappiness.

His girlfriend sued him for part of the winnings and won. Countless relatives badgered him relentlessly for gifts and loans. Then, in an almost unthinkable turn of events, his own brother hired a hit man to kill him in an effort to get everything poor Bud had left.

Within a year, Bud was completely broke—and $1 million in debt.[24]

Money, it turns out, is hardly the key to happiness or purpose in life. If we aren't careful, a love of money can get in the way of hearing from God. Do you remember that Jesus ran into a young man with this problem? This young man had a lot going for him. He really seemed to want to live a life that pleased God. The very question of his eternal destiny was what had brought him to Jesus.

"Teacher," he asked Jesus, "what good thing must I do to get eternal life?" (Matthew 19:16).

Jesus took a good long at him and loved him enough to pinpoint the one thing that was getting in the way of this young man's relationship with God: his abundance.

"Go, sell your possessions and give to the poor, and you will have treasures in heaven. Then come, follow me" (v. 21).

This was a personal invitation to follow Christ, but the young man couldn't do it. He couldn't let go of his wealth. Scripture tells us he turned around and "went away sad" (v. 22).

This story isn't included in Scripture to suggest that having money is bad. It is a warning not to make it our first love. It's so easy for us to hold our stuff too tightly. If we aren't careful, we'll find ourselves consumed by the fear that there won't be enough or that we will lose what we have. Then, before we know it, we have a dangerous idol on the throne of our lives.

The stories of Bud Post and the rich young ruler serve as

warnings never to allow what we have or what we fear we'll lose to drown out the voice of God, our true Provider.

Take a few minutes to bring this issue before the Lord. With the psalmist, pray, "Search me, God" (Psalm 139:23). Let's make sure we don't let anything get in the way of the voice of God.

> *Whether I have much or little, I will trust in God as my Provider and treasure Him most.*

ꙮ Five Minutes in the Word ꙮ

Do not be overawed when others grow rich, when the splendor of their houses increases; for they will take nothing with them when they die, their splendor will not descend with them.

Psalm 49:16–17

The name of the LORD is a fortified tower; the righteous run to it and are safe. The wealth of the rich is their fortified city; they imagine it a wall too high to scale.

Proverbs 18:10–11

People who have wealth but lack understanding
are like the beasts that perish.

Psalm 49:20

"Where your treasure is, there your heart will be also."

Luke 12:34

Do not wear yourself out to get rich; do not trust your own
cleverness. Cast but a glance at riches, and they are gone, for
they will surely sprout wings and fly off to the sky like an eagle.

Proverbs 23:4–5

Our Picture of God

I wish I could believe everything you said tonight."

I looked into the eyes of this young woman who had waited until the crowd was almost gone. I wondered what her story was.

"What are you struggling to believe?" I asked her.

"You said that God wants us to come to Him as we are," she said. "How can you say that when you don't know our stories?"

"It's not so much about our stories," I said. "It's about God's story."

We took a walk and talked for quite a while that evening. It became clear that this lovely young woman had never—in any relationship—experienced the kind of love and acceptance that God lavishes on us. She was used to being judged and considered not good enough. And she had projected those judgmental, critical attitudes onto God.

That young woman is not alone in her thinking. I have talked with enough believers to know that a lot of us struggle with one or another misconception about God. We might say the right things about Him—that He is good and kind—but deep down, we wonder if He really receives us without condemnation. The sad thing is that if we really believe God is cruel and condemning, we *will* pull away from Him. Like Adam and Eve in the moments after the fall, we will hide.

So what can we do if we find ourselves pulling away from God because we fear His condemnation?

We can ask Him to heal that wound in us and replace our misconceptions with the reality that He is a good and loving God, the One who forgives us and has paid the price for our sin through the blood of His Son.

We can also immerse ourselves in the truth of Scripture that tells us who He is! And what exactly does the Bible say about God's heart for us? It says He is compassionate and gracious, slow to anger, faithful and loving (Psalm 86:15). The Bible tells us our God is merciful (Luke 6:36) and kind (Ephesians 2:7). It says He is patient and good too (2 Peter 3:9; Psalm 109:21).

When you find a verse that corrects your misconceptions or speaks powerfully to your heart, write it out and keep it somewhere close where you can see it often. Bit by bit, your heavenly Father will use the truth of Scripture to establish in your mind and heart an accurate image of who He is.

As you realize the truth about who God really is, you will find it easier to open your heart to Him. Soon you will even find yourself running into His presence instead of shrinking away in fear.

Let God begin to restore His image in your heart today!

> *God stands with open arms and says,*
> *"I love you . . . come as you are!"*

ᴖᴗ Five Minutes in the Word ᴖᴗ

You, Lord, are a compassionate and gracious God, slow
to anger, abounding in love and faithfulness.
Psalm 86:15

God raised us up with Christ and seated us with him in
the heavenly realms in Christ Jesus, in order that in the
coming ages he might show the incomparable riches of his
grace, expressed in his kindness to us in Christ Jesus.
Ephesians 2:6–7

The Lord is not slow in keeping his promise, as some
understand slowness. Instead he is patient with you, not
wanting anyone to perish, but everyone to come to repentance.

2 Peter 3:9

You, Sovereign Lord, help me for your name's sake;
out of the goodness of your love, deliver me.

Psalm 109:21

"The Lord, the Lord, the compassionate and
gracious God, slow to anger, abounding in love
and faithfulness, maintaining love to thousands,
and forgiving wickedness, rebellion and sin."

Exodus 34:6–7

Love is patient, love is kind. It does not envy, it
does not boast, it is not proud. It does not dishonor
others, it is not self-seeking, it is not easily angered,
it keeps no record of wrongs. Love does not delight
in evil but rejoices with the truth. It always protects,
always trusts, always hopes, always perseveres.

1 Corinthians 13:4–7

So Many Bright and Shining Distractions

In the powerful closing chapters of C. S. Lewis's The Chronicles of Narnia series, the old Narnia in all its wonder and beauty was being swept away to make way for the new Narnia, perfect and eternal. The kings and queens of old had all been called back to Narnia from earth so they might forever rule in paradise with Aslan.

All except one. One queen was missing.

"Where is Queen Susan?" Tirian asked.

"My sister Susan," answered Peter shortly and gravely, "is no longer a friend of Narnia."

"Oh Susan!" said Jill. "She's interested in nothing nowadays except nylons and lipstick and invitations."

Susan, it seems, was so captivated by the lovely things of this world that when the moment came for her to permanently take her place as queen in the new Narnia, she could no longer hear Aslan's call.[25]

Just like Susan, we are so easily distracted by a world that is filled to the brim with things to do, places to go, and amazing things to see. Even on a recent trip to one of the poorest barrios in the Dominican Republic, I saw satellite dishes on corrugated iron roofs. Western entertainment was flooding into homes that often struggled to put food on the table.

Is it any wonder we find it challenging to hear the still, small voice of God when we are surrounded by so many bright and shiny distractions, so many buttons to push, so many screens to swipe and posts to like?

If you're like me, there have been times when you've picked up your phone or turned on the television planning to spend just a few minutes in front of the screen, only to be shocked later by how much time had slipped right by.

Now, this isn't about condemnation. It is about taking a few minutes to think about how distracting our world can be and choosing to protect our time with the Father. Too many times I've finally gotten myself to shut off the phone or television, wishing I had spent my time differently. But I have never regretted a single second I have spent in the presence of my heavenly Father.

I'm sure the same goes for you. So today, choose to spend time with the One who will bring you more joy and peace than anything else in this world.

> *The light of Christ shines brighter*
> *than anything this world has to offer.*

∼◌ Five Minutes in the Word ◌∼

Better is one day in your courts than a thousand
elsewhere; I would rather be a doorkeeper in the house
of my God than dwell in the tents of the wicked.

Psalm 84:10

Blessed are the people who know the joyful sound! They walk, O
Lord, in the light of Your countenance. In Your name they rejoice
all day long, and in Your righteousness they are exalted.

Psalm 89:15–16 NKJV

Turn my eyes away from worthless things;
preserve my life according to your word.

Psalm 119:37

Blessed are those you choose and bring near to live in your courts! We
are filled with the good things of your house, of your holy temple.

Psalm 65:4

"Do not store up for yourselves treasures on earth, where moths and vermin destroy, and where thieves break in and steal. But store up for yourselves treasures in heaven, where moths and vermin do not destroy, and where thieves do not break in and steal. For where your treasure is, there your heart will be also."

Matthew 6:19–21

Oh, how I love your law! I meditate on it all day long.

Psalm 119:97

A Broken Vessel

Gene Cooley knows all too well the life-wrecking power of gossip.

Life was going pretty well. Gene had a job he enjoyed, and he was engaged to be married. Then one night tragedy struck: his fiancée was killed. The grief over the devastating loss of the woman he loved would have been enough for any man to deal with, but Gene's pain was compounded by rumors that began circulating online in the days following her death. An anonymous person had accused him of being addicted to drugs and complicit in his fiancée's death. None of the accusations were true, but the damage had been done. Gene was ostracized in his hometown, and when his boss heard the rumors, he lost his job. One person's cruel words came very close to destroying Gene's life.[26]

David—the shepherd, psalmist, and king—knew this kind of pain; he had been the subject of some malicious slander. In Psalm 31, he poured out his broken heart to God: "I am forgotten like a dead man, out of mind; I am like a broken vessel" (v. 12 NKJV).

The words *broken vessel* don't have the same impact on us that they did on David. In his day the ground was littered with pottery shards and pieces of broken vessels. Once a piece of pottery was cracked, it was no longer of any use at all. It was simply thrown out. It shattered on the ground, and its pieces became part of the landscape. There was no repairing a broken piece of pottery; it was utterly and forever ruined.

In the wake of vicious gossip, that is how David felt about his life: utterly ruined and beyond repair. So he turned to the only One who could help. David needed to hear from God. He needed to hear words of comfort. Words of restoration. He knew that his God was the only One who could put his broken heart back together again.

Have you ever been a victim of the rumor mill? Have someone's words left you feeling that your life is damaged beyond repair? I know what that feels like. When I was hospitalized for clinical depression, all sorts of stories circulated suggesting I was anything from a pathological liar to someone who should never have been trusted. In my brokenness I turned to Jesus and discovered that, rather than throwing the pieces away, He makes something whole and beautiful with them.

Trust that He will do the same for you!

> **God is in the business of healing broken hearts.**

✦ Five Minutes in the Word ✦

The righteous person may have many troubles,
but the LORD delivers him from them all.

Psalm 34:19

The Lord stood at my side and gave me strength, so that through
me the message might be fully proclaimed and all the Gentiles
might hear it. And I was delivered from the lion's mouth. The Lord
will rescue me from every evil attack and will bring me safely to his
heavenly kingdom. To him be the glory ever and ever. Amen.

2 Timothy 4:17–18

He has sent me to . . . proclaim freedom for the
captives and release from darkness for the prisoners,
to proclaim the year of the LORD's favor and the day of
vengeance of our God, to comfort all who mourn.
Isaiah 61:1–2

He heals the brokenhearted and binds up their wounds.
Psalm 147:3

Praise be to the God and Father of our Lord Jesus Christ, the
Father of compassion and the God of all comfort, who comforts
us in all our troubles, so that we can comfort those in any
trouble with the comfort we ourselves receive from God.
2 Corinthians 1:3–4

The LORD comforts his people and will
have compassion on his afflicted ones.
Isaiah 49:13

Running Strong

I am not much of a runner unless I'm chasing one of my renegade escapee dogs, but there is something about marathons that I really love. It's those inspirational signs people hold up along the route with sayings like, "Focus on how far you've run, not how far you have to go." Or, "Warning! Awesome sense of accomplishment ahead!"

My favorite marathon signs of all time were worn on the backs of three friends who were running together. Each young woman had pinned a sign of encouragement to her back for the runners who were behind them. The first one said, "You are EPIC! Have a great race!" The next friend's sign read, "Pain is temporary. Quitting is forever." The last young woman's sign declared, "Yes, you can do it." I don't know who these ladies are, but I love them!

We all need a voice of encouragement like theirs in our lives. I am so thankful that when my courage runs short and my strength is gone, I can find fresh encouragement for my journey at the feet of my Savior.

And I am not alone. Scripture is filled with the stories of great men and women of faith who needed an encouraging word from the Lord when they found their strength spent and their knees shaking. Moses felt that way when God gave him orders to lead Israel to freedom from Egypt. Joshua was in the same position just before the children of God entered the promised land. And think of Queen Esther—one of my favorites—who was divinely placed on the throne at the very moment the children of Israel were facing genocide. As she faced the possibility of losing her own life in the effort to save her family and friends, God spoke through her uncle to give her strength to go the next mile. "Who knows," he said, "but that you have come to your royal position for such a time as this?" (Esther 4:14).

This life isn't a sprint. It's a marathon. There are going to be days when the miles stretch long and we feel like there is no way we can make it to the finish line. That is why we need to hear from the Lord each step of the way and receive fresh encouragement for the journey.

And that truth reminds me of one other marathon sign I love, one that is pretty solid advice for running the race of faith: "When your legs get tired, run with your heart."

A heart that has sought the Savior will find refreshment, strength, and encouragement for the miles ahead.

> *When your soul gets tired, remember your Savior will sustain you.*

～ぐ～ Five Minutes in the Word ～Ɔ～

"Do not fear, for I am with you, do not be dismayed, for I am your God. I will strengthen you and help you; I will uphold you with my righteous right hand."
Isaiah 41:10

Be on your guard; stand firm in the faith; be courageous; be strong.
1 Corinthians 16:13

Let us not become weary in doing good, for at the proper time we will reap a harvest if we do not give up.
Galatians 6:9

Brothers and sisters, I do not consider myself yet to have taken hold of it. But one thing I do: Forgetting what is behind and straining toward what is ahead, I press on toward the goal to win the prize for which God has called me heavenward in Christ Jesus.

Philippians 3:13–14

I have fought the good fight, I have finished the race, I have kept the faith. Now there is in store for me the crown of righteousness, which the Lord, the righteous Judge, will award me on that day—and not only to me, but also to all who have longed for his appearing.

2 Timothy 4:7–8

Keep My Lamp Burning

The oldest lighthouse in the United States, Boston Light, first cast its hopeful glow over the harbor in 1716. The light source has changed and improved over the years, advancing from tallow candles to whale oil, then to lard oil, and then kerosene. Lighthouse keepers even used cabbage oil for a time! But one thing has remained the same: a lighthouse keeper always lives on the little outcropping of rock and faithfully keeps the light burning.

Today Boston Light boasts the only Coast Guard lighthouse keeper left in the United States, and her name is Sally Snowman. Sally is the seventieth keeper of the Boston Light, and her stint marks the end of an era.

Sally most certainly knows, as did all other lighthouse keepers before her, this truth: to give light away, the fire must first be lit and then maintained.[27]

First John 1:5 describes Jesus' presence in this world as a light that penetrated the darkness. Even today, as His followers and ambassadors, we are to be bearers of His light in the hope that those who are lost might safely find their way home to His great love. Nothing can ever take the light of Christ from us, but if we neglect it, the flame becomes dim.

One way we can ensure that our lights keep burning brightly is to simply spend time with Jesus, allowing Him to reignite our hearts with His love. When we take time to rest in His presence, we find ourselves renewed and able to shine hope and truth into a world that is helplessly lost in a sea of despair.

Do you ever get just plain worn-out? It's okay to take time for yourself to rest and refuel. Find a quiet place, even for five minutes, to take a deep breath and remind yourself of the love Christ has for you.

A world in need is counting on us to keep shining the light of Jesus' love. Let's take time with Him to be sure that light keeps shining brightly!

> *Let Jesus fill you with the light of*
> *His love so all can see the way to Him.*

৵৻ Five Minutes in the Word ৵৴

The light shines in the darkness, and the darkness has not overcome it.

John 1:5

You are all children of the light and children of the day.
We do not belong to the night or to the darkness.

1 Thessalonians 5:5

[Give] thanks to the Father, who has qualified you to share in the
inheritance of his holy people in the kingdom of light. For he has rescued
us from the dominion of darkness and brought us into the kingdom of
the Son he loves, in whom we have redemption, the forgiveness of sins.

Colossians 1:12–14

All this is from God, who reconciled us to himself through Christ and
gave us the ministry of reconciliation: that God was reconciling the
world to himself in Christ, not counting people's sins against them.
And he has committed to us the message of reconciliation. We are
therefore Christ's ambassadors, as though God were making his appeal
through us. We implore you on Christ's behalf: Be reconciled to God.

2 Corinthians 5:18–20

You, LORD, keep my lamp burning; my God turns my darkness into light.

Psalm 18:28

Practicing Forgiveness

When I was teaching in a church in the Midwest, the leaders asked if I would allow a time for questions and answers after my final session. I was more than happy to. I always find the kinds of questions women ask fascinating.

"Where did you get your shoes?"

"Is that your natural hair color?"

Many of the questions that day made me smile, but one was about as important a question as we can ever ask.

"What do you think is the greatest hindrance to spiritual growth?"

My answer was simple: unforgiveness.

A lack of forgiveness can be a huge hindrance to our ability to hear from God and therefore to our spiritual growth. Like a fortress of hurt, unforgiveness stands between our heart and God's. It is such a serious matter that Jesus directly linked our forgiveness of others to His forgiveness of us (Matthew 6:15).

He also addressed unforgiveness in an important way in Matthew 5:23–24: "If you are offering your gift at the altar and there remember that your brother or sister has something against you, leave your gift there in front of the altar. First go and be reconciled to them; then come and offer your gift."

Wow. So if there is a relationship that needs reconciling in your life, Jesus says to "leave your gift there in front of the altar" and go deal with that relationship. It's important for our relationship with God that we forgive one another.

Now, I am not pretending for even a minute that forgiveness is easy or that life is fair. (I've often said to my son, "Fair doesn't live here, but Jesus does.") And sometimes, even when you forgive another person, you may find that they are just too dangerous for you to be around very much, if at all!

Bottom line, what I am challenging you to do is trust God with the hurt of your past. The ability to forgive is God's gift, helping us live in a world that's not fair. So give up on the goal of exacting justice and instead surrender the situation to your just and kind God.

You may not be able to trust the person who hurt you, but you can always trust your Father in heaven. It is this truth that makes forgiveness possible.

And the sooner you reconcile with your brother or sister, the sooner you can get back to that gift you left at the altar and sweet fellowship with the Lover of your soul.

Don't wait another minute. Practice forgiveness today.

> *The gift of forgiveness—of being forgiven*
> *and of forgiving—will set you free!*

❧ Five Minutes in the Word ❧

Bear with each other and forgive one another if any of you has
a grievance against someone. Forgive as the Lord forgave you.

Colossians 3:13

"Forgive us our sins, for we also forgive everyone who
sins against us. And lead us not into temptation."

Luke 11:4

"Do not judge, and you will not be judged. Do not condemn, and you will not be condemned. Forgive, and you will be forgiven."

Luke 6:37

"When you stand praying, if you hold anything against anyone, forgive him, so that your Father in heaven may forgive you your sins."

Mark 11:25

"'Love the Lord your God with all your heart and with all your soul and with all your mind.' This is the first and greatest commandment. And the second is like it: 'Love your neighbor as yourself.'"

Matthew 22:37–39

When the Lights Go Out

I think one of God's greatest mercies to us is this: each and every day, the sun sets.

This gift is more difficult to recognize now than it was a couple hundred years ago. Back then, before the invention of modern lighting, the day was done at sunset. It was time to put work away until the next day, time to make peace with all the tasks left undone and any mistakes made.

In the twenty-first century, though, we can delay that process. We extend the working hours late into the night, or we let flickering screens make us numb to any disappointments from the day.

But eventually, the lights do go out.

I hope with all my heart that those moments are peaceful for you, but I know that's not always the case. Is there something that troubles you when the lights go out?

Mistakes you have made . . .

Items on your to-do list left undone . . .

A broken heart . . .

Worries . . .

Fear . . .

I understand. I have been in each of those places too.

But here is what I have discovered: those long night hours are transformed when I turn to the presence of my God who loves me. There I find every mistake I have made and every regret that haunts me swallowed up in the ocean of His endless grace. My "not enough" is no match for God's awesome power, and He is infinitely gentle with my broken heart.

And as for fear . . . what do I have to fear when the Lord of hosts watches over me while I sleep?

The psalmist knew this truth. Have you ever read Psalm 91? It's a wonderful one to read before going to sleep. I especially love these verses: "Do not be afraid of the terrors of the night, nor the arrow that flies in the day. Do not dread the disease that stalks in darkness, nor the disaster that strikes at midday. . . . I will rescue those who love me. I will protect those who trust in my name" (vv. 5–6, 14 NLT).

Tonight, as you turn out the light, turn your heart to

your loving Father. Then rest in the promise that He is keeping watch over you all night long.

> *Lie down and rest, for the Lord is with you.*

～⌒ Five Minutes in the Word ⌒～

*Praise the LORD, all you servants of the LORD who
minister by night in the house of the LORD. Lift up
your hands in the sanctuary and praise the LORD.*
Psalm 134:1–2

I lie down and sleep; I wake again, because the LORD sustains me.
Psalm 3:5

Into your hands I commit my spirit; deliver me, LORD, my faithful God.
Psalm 31:5

*In peace I will lie down and sleep, for you alone,
LORD, make me dwell in safety.*
Psalm 4:8

God's Delight

When Christian was a little boy, one of my favorite things to do after he was tucked in bed and we'd said our prayers was to kiss him good night, go to his bedroom door, and stop. Then I'd turn around and ask him, "Which boy does Mommy love?" He would put his little hand on his cheek and answer, "This boy!" Then he would lie down with a big grin on his face.

It's wonderful to be loved, wouldn't you say? But perhaps you can't speak from experience; maybe that doesn't describe your life. If you haven't felt loved, then my heart aches for you more than I know how to put words on paper. But I also have some really good news for you: God is absolutely in love with you!

And God wants you to know that He has never left you for a moment, that He loves you enough to send His Son to die for you, and that He rejoices over you. In other words, God delights in you.

Read that again: God *delights* in *you*.

God delights in His children! That truth is almost too much to absorb, isn't it? I think a lot of Christians struggle to believe this. Maybe you are one of them. Perhaps you think, *I know God loves me . . . but delights in me? Me?*

Yes, you! It is absolutely true! God delights in you, and if you are like me, you need to hear that truth often. You need Him to whisper it in the morning when you first open your eyes and again a little while later when you have already taken a few hard hits to the heart. You need to hear Him tell you He delights in you when you bow your head over the evening meal, and you need those words to be the last ones you hear as you drift off to sleep.

In a world that takes so much from us, oh, how we need to hear our Father say that He *delights* in us!

Don't wait. Open your heart to Him now . . . and then over and over again. Your heavenly Father will never grow tired of telling you . . .

"I *delight* in you!"

The next time you catch your reflection in a mirror, ask yourself this question, "Which girl does Jesus love?" Then put your hand on your cheek and say with confidence, "This girl!"

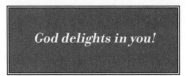

God delights in you!

⮜⮜ Five Minutes in the Word ⮞⮞

The LORD delights in those who fear him,
who put their hope in his unfailing love.

Psalm 147:11

Keep me as the apple of your eye; hide me in the shadow of your wings.

Psalm 17:8

The LORD loves justice, and he will never abandon the godly. He will
keep them safe forever, but the children of the wicked will die.

Psalm 37:28 NLT

The LORD was my support. He brought me out into a
spacious place; he rescued me because he delighted in me.

Psalm 18:18–19

Your works are wonderful, I know that full well.

Psalm 139:14

Notes

1. Robert J. Morgan, *Nelson's Complete Book of Stories, Illustrations & Quotes* (Nashville: Thomas Nelson, 2000), 152.
2. Sarah Butler, "The Chilean Miners' Miracles: How Faith Helped Them Survive," *CNN*, August 4, 2015, http://www.cnn.com /2015/08/02/world/chilean-miners-miracles/index.html.
3. *Cast Away*—Official Movie Trailer, MovieBout.com, *YouTube*, July 28, 2012, https://youtube.com/watch?v=VfXpFgyAY_U.
4. Max Lucado, *You Are Special* (Wheaton, IL: Crossway Books, 1997), 15, 25–26.
5. "The Heart Wants What It Wants," *This American Life*, October 30, 2015, episode 571.
6. Roswell D. Hitchcock, *Hitchcock's Bible Names Dictionary* (Cedar Rapids, IA: Laridian, 2015), s.v. "Leah."
7. Scott Neuman, "On the Anniversary of Apollo 8, How the 'Earthrise' Photo Was Made," *Morning Edition*, *NPR*, December 23, 2013, http://www.npr.org/sections/thetwo way/2013/12/23/256 605845/on-anniversary-of-apollo-8-how-the-earthrise-photo -was-made.
8. NASA, "Apollo 8: Earthrise," last updated June 25, 2013, http:// www.nasa.gov/multimedia/imagegallery/image_feature_1249 .html.
9. J. Alec Motyer, *Isaiah* (Downers Grove, IL: IVP Academic, 2009), 453.

10. Morgan, 546.

11. *Advanced English Dictionary*, version 9.0, 2015, s.v. "meditation."

12. A. W. Tozer, *We Travel an Appointed Way*, ed. Harry Verploegh (Camp Hill, PA: Wing Spread Publishers, 1988).

13. Ibid., 57.

14. "Saint Francis of Assisi Biography," Biography.com, last updated June 23, 2015, http://www.biography.com/people/st-francis-of-assisi-21152679#death-and-legacy.

15. Nina Siegal, "Where van Gogh Comes to Life," *New York Times*, Travel Section, December 27, 2015, 1, 8–9.

16. Morgan, 744.

17. Rebecca J. Rosen, "America's Workers: Stressed Out, Overwhelmed, and Totally Exhausted," *The Atlantic*, March 25, 2014, http://www.theatlantic.com/business/archive/2014/03/americas-workers-stressed-out-overwhelmed-totally-exhausted/284615/.

18. Abraham Joshua Heschel, *The Sabbath* (New York: Farrar, Straus, and Giroux, 1979), 13.

19. Essena O'Neill Ikaryn, "Why I REALLY Am Quitting Social Media," YouTube, November 3, 2015, https://www.youtube.com/watch?v=Xe1Qyks8QEM.

20. Mary Oliver, *Long Life: Essays and Other Writings* (Cambridge: Da Capo Press, 2004), 11.

21. "Her Story," Trafficking Hope Louisiana, updated January 26, 2016, http://www.traffickinghopela.org/hope-updates/.

22. "3-Year-Old Mateo Makes His Case for Cupcakes: 'Linda, Honey, Just Listen,'" The Big Tino Network, *YouTube*, March 10, 2014, https://www.youtube.com/watch?v=TP8RB7UZHKI.

23. Die Befreier, "The Liberators: Why We Fought," *History* (Germany), *YouTube*, April 29, 2015, https://youtube.com/watch?v=XwuQto OyvOo.

24. Mandi Woodruff and Michael B. Kelley, "19 Lottery Winners Who Blew It All," *Business Inside*, May 19, 2013, http://www.businessinsider.com/17 -lottery-winners-who-blew-it-all-2013–5.

25. C. S. Lewis, *The Last Battle* (New York: HarperCollins, 1956), 54.

26. Eamon McNiff, "Innocent Man's Life Destroyed by Anonymous Topix Poster," *ABC News*, March 21, 2012, http://abcnews.go.com/Technology/topix-innocent -mans-life-destroyed-anonymous-online-poster/story?id=15963310.

27. Sally Snowman (Keeper of Boston Light), in phone interview with the author, February 10, 2015.

Want to take 5 more?

The entire 5 Minutes with Jesus series
is available at bookstores everywhere.

Visit 5MinutesWithJesus.com to view
exclusive content and share inspiration!

Connect: